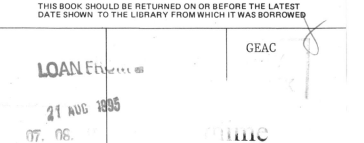

S

A

A

Paul Reakes

S.
Ne

5.25

CHARACTERS

Vileun the Vile, evil Usurper of the Universe
Astra, the Astrologer
Null
Void } Vileun's Astro-nuts
Little Tommy Tucker
Dame Dangle
Roberta, the Robot
Professor Atnas, really Santa Claus
Captain Dick Daring
Crystal, a visitor from the North Pole
The Dancing Doll
The Leader of the Varborites
The Monster of the Wilderlands
Prince Paragon of Varbos
Chorus, of **Villagers, Village Children and Varborites**

ACT ONE

SCENE 1   Vileun's Domain on the Planet Varbos
SCENE 2   The Village of Merrydale, Earth
SCENE 3   Another Part of the Village
SCENE 4   A Room in Santa's House

ACT TWO

SCENE 1   In Outer Space
SCENE 2   Vileun's Palace on Varbos
SCENE 3   The Wilderlands of Varbos
SCENE 4   Vileun's Palace
FINALE   The Village of Merrydale

MUSIC PLOT

ACT I

Song and Dance	**Tommy, Village Children and Villagers**
Comedy Song	**Dame Dangle with Tommy and Village Children**
Solo Dance	**Roberta**
Song	**Dick with Dame, Tommy and Village Children**
Song and Dance	**Dame, Dick, Crystal, Santa, Roberta, Tommy, Village Children and Villagers**
Audience Participation Song	**Null and Void**
Duet	**Dick and Crystal**
Solo Dance	**The Dancing Doll**
Song and Dance	**Dick, Crystal, Dame, Roberta, Tommy, Village Children and Villagers**

ACT II

Song and Dance	**Tommy, Roberta, Village Children and Villagers**
Song	**Dick and Crystal with Tommy, Roberta, Village Children and Villagers**
Comedy Song	**Dame Dangle**
Audience Participation Song	**Dame, Null and Void**
Dance	**The Varborites**
Comedy Solo Dance	**The Monster**
Song	**Crystal with Dick, Roberta, Tommy, Village Children and Villagers**
Reprise of Song	**All**
We wish you a Merry Christmas	**Full Company**

PRODUCTION NOTES

The pantomime offers opportunities for elaborate staging, but can be produced quite simply if facilities are limited. There are four full sets:

The Village of Merrydale
A Room in Santa's House
Interior of the Rocket
The Wilderlands of Varbos

These scenes are interlinked by tabs or front cloth scenes.

The Flying Saucer can be very elaborate if facilities allow. If overhead space and facilities are limited, a well painted hardboard cut-out, lowered on strong lines, will serve the purpose. This can be made in two sections, one behind the other. As the main section of the saucer descends, the lower part can slide down from behind it, giving the impression of a landing stage.

The Magic Cabinet is a revolving box built on a turntable. One side shows a traditional magic cabinet with practical door. The other side shows a shining space rocket with practical door. The box must be deep enough to house the Dancing Doll. A black curtain divides the interior of the box into two sections. This curtain conceals the Dancing Doll until she is ready for her appearance. During the black-out the box is turned to show the rocket side.

DESCRIPTION OF CHARACTERS AND COSTUMES

Vileun is a black-hearted villain whose only aim in life is to become the Supreme Master of the Universe. His villainy must never flag, he must be hated by the cast and audience right up to the final curtain. Ideally he should be tall and thin with curling eyebrows and a black pointed beard. His costume and make-up should be magnificently evil "Outer Space".

Astra is Vileun's henchwoman, a zany villainess. Her "trance" scenes should be played comedy dramatic and with great relish. Her costume, make-up and hairstyle should be very bizarre with astronomical signs very much in evidence.

Null and **Void** are a sort of "outer space" version of the traditional broker's men parts. Even though they work for Vileun this should not be held against them, they are just a couple of stupid, but lovable aliens. **Null** is the more intelligent of the two — but only slightly. **Void** is a cuddly nitwit. They should wear comic outer space uniforms with perhaps green faces and large ears.

Little Tommy Tucker (*Child's part*) is a cheeky little chap who takes great delight in ribbing Dame Dangle. His costume should be slightly more outstanding than the other children.

Dame Dangle is a lovable old girl who changes her moods at the drop of a hat. She should be on very friendly terms with the audience, especially the youngsters. Her Act I costume is of the traditional petticoats, apron and bonnet variety. In Act II she wears an outrageous red, white and blue space costume, which makes her look like a cross between Wonder Woman and an astronaut.

Roberta (*Child's part*) is an all-talking, all-singing, all-dancing, perky little Robot with ariels and a "beep". Her movements are jerky and her voice is definitely "Dalek" in tone. Her costume can be as elaborate as possible, remembering that easy movement is essential. It is box shaped with flexible tubing covering arms and legs. A separate box covers the head with an aperture for her little silver face to peer through. The "beep" can be spoken, or a special "beeper" could be concealed in the costume and operated by a button in the palm of Roberta's gloved hand.

Professor Atnas is really **Santa Claus** in disguise. He must be played as a real person, a kindly, human old gent, not a "grotto" Santa. His white hair and beard must look real, no cotton wool hooked over the ears, please. A description of the costume he wears as the Professor is given in the script. His red, fur trimmed Santa Claus suit should be of the short coat variety with boots, cap, etc.

Captain Dick Daring (*Principal Boy*) should be the most dashing, courageous soldier ever to don fishnet tights. He must be the perfect hero throughout. He is resplendent in a "Quality Street" style uniform, cap and boots.

Crystal (*Principal Girl*) is Santa's beautiful young assistant at the North Pole. She should be enchanting, almost fairy-like. Her costume should reflect the part of the world she comes from, perhaps a white dress with fur trimmed silver cloak and hood.

The Dancing Doll must be a good solo dancer. Her costume, make-up and hair must be an exact copy of the rag doll carried by the 1st Girl.

The Leader of the Varborites is a small, but very important role as he/she tells us all about Prince Paragon's downfall.

The Monster of the Wilderlands can be a solo part, or played by two or three persons in the style of a panto dragon. The costume should be comically hideous, a costume designer's dream—or nightmare. However elaborate the head gear, the actor inside must be able to see and speak clearly.

Prince Paragon of Varbos (*Female/male or child*) is a very small part but should be played with great dignity and a spectacular "outer space" royal costume.

The Village Children are by no means just "dressing". They all have lines to speak and participate in lots of the action and musical numbers. Although the script calls for only twelve children—six boys (counting Tommy Tucker) and six girls—more can be used if so desired. Their costumes should be picturesque and colourful, with a definite leaning towards Dickensian.

The Varborites only appear in Act II but are very important to the story. They can be played by adults or, better still, by a mixed chorus of adults and children. Their costumes and make-up should be fantastically "Outer Space".

The **Adult Chorus** appear in Act I as **Villagers, Farmhands, Milkmaids** etc., their bright, picturesque costumes befitting the rustic scene. In Act II, if so desired, half of them can remain as **Villagers** and the other half can play **Varborites**. If a large chorus is available, however, they can remain as two separate groups.

ACT I

Vileun's Domain on the Planet Varbos

Tabs, or a front cloth, showing the forbidding interior of Vileun's space palace. Strange lighting and weird background noises to create a sinister atmosphere. A little ground mist will add to the effect if facilities allow

Vileun the Vile enters

Vileun (*laughing demoniacally*) Ha! Ha! Ha! My plan to conquer the Universe is almost complete. Each planet will soon be under my control! Oh, what an ingenious plan. A plan that will make me, Vileun the Vile, supreme Master of the Galaxy. Ha! Ha! Ha! It's such a simple plan too. On each planet there is a nasty little species known as *children*! They are the most *obnoxious, odious* little creatures imaginable! I hate 'em all! (*He invites audience participation*) Each planet contains certain things that make these little brats happy. Toys! Games! Sweets, and such like! Well, I have taken away these things. So now the children are very miserable! Consequently, all the grown ups are miserable too! It seems they like to see their wretched offsprings enjoying themselves. So now I, Vileun the Vile, have them in my power. I will only return these things if each planet accepts me as its Lord and Master! Ha! Ha! Ha! Oh, I'm clever! Don't you think I'm clever?

Audience participation

Well, I am! So there! I'm so clever I could hug myself. I think I will. (*He hugs himself*) Oo! You clever boy!

Astra the Astrologer enters. She carries a report, a chart of the planets and a large black book

Astra (*coughing*) Ahmmm!
Vileun Ah, Astra, the Astrologer!
Astra (*bowing*) O, Vileun, Vilest of Viles, I crave an audience.
Vileun (*pointing to the audience*) Well, you have one! And a pretty rotten lot they are!

Audience participation

Well, Astra, have you come to tell me how my conquest of the Universe is progressing?

Astra I have, your Evilness. Here is the latest report.

Vileun Read it!

Astra (*reading*) On Pluto, all the Pepsi pools have been poisoned.

Vileun Perfect!

Astra On Mars, all the Mars Bars have been melted.

Vileun Marvellous!

Astra On Saturn, all the Space Invaders have been sabotaged.

Vileun Splendid!

Astra On Venus, all the videos have been vandalized.

Vileun Very good!

Astra On Mercury, all the "Murphys" have been munched.

Vileun Magnificent!

Astra On Jupiter, all the jellies have been jinxed.

Vileun Joy!

Astra On Neptune, all the nougat has been nicked.

Vileun Nice one!

Astra On Uranus ...

Vileun I beg your pardon!

Astra Uranus—the planet.

Vileun Oh, yes. Carry on.

Astra On Uranus, all the umbrellas are upside down.

Vileun Utter bliss! Ha! Ha! Ha! I now have complete control of all the planets! It is time to issue my terms! (*To Astra*) Send a message to each planet stating that I, Vileun the Vile, will only return these things to normal if they accept me as their supreme ruler. If they refuse they will never see their miserable children happy again! Go!

Astra But ...

Vileun Did you not hear my order!

Astra Yes, your Nastiness, but ... but you've forgotten a planet.

Vileun What! Impossible! Which one?

Astra Earth.

Vileun Earth? Earth? Never heard of it! There's no such planet! (*To audience*) Is there?

Audience participation. "Oh, no there isn't"—"Oh, yes, there is", etc.

Well *I've* never heard of it!

Astra (*showing him the chart*) It's on the chart, your Stubbornness. Look!

Vileun (*looking*) Is *that* it? (*He points to the chart*)

Astra No, your Silliness! That's a bit of "Cosmic Crunch" I had for breakfast. (*She flicks the crumb away*) There it is! (*She points*)

Vileun (*peering*) Earth! Ha! What a puny little planet! No wonder I overlooked it. But, no matter how small, it shall not escape Vileun the Vile! It must be brought in line with the others. We must find out at once what makes the children on Earth happy! Let me look at your Thesauras!

Astra (*coyly*) Oo! Your Rudeness!

Vileun The *book*, you Galactic Geriatric! (*He grabs the book and thumbs through it*) Earth . . . Earth . . . Ah! Here it is! (*He reads*) "Earth is round and has green bits and blue bits . . ." Bah! . . . Ah! Here is something! (*He reads*) "Each year, in the Earth month of December, the inhabitants of this planet celebrate—Christmas."

Vileun and Astra exchange puzzled looks. Vileun continues reading

"This is a time for much eating, drinking and the consuming of *Alka-Seltzer*?" (*He is puzzled, then continues reading*) "Christmas is essentially a time for the *young* Earthlings . . ." (*To Astra*) Ah! Ha! (*Reading*) "An elusive old man, known as Santa Claus, travels the entire planet distributing toys and presents to the young." (*He snaps the book shut with a bang*) Ha! Ha! Great slithering slabs of slime! That's it! I must *stop* this Santa Claus.

Astra How, your Craftiness?

Vileun By going to Earth and kidnapping him!

Astra But how will you find him? The book gives no details.

Vileun *You* will find him. You must go into one of your trances.

Astra But . . . But I haven't been well, your Selfishness. Not since I had that bout of the Venutian Vapours!

Vileun I command it!

Astra Oh, very well! (*She throws the book etc. to the floor and proceeds to put herself into a trance. This she does with lots of swaying about, wailing and comic business. In a trance*) Ooo! Ooo! I can see the planet Earth. Oo! I am passing over a piece of land known as England. Ooo! It grows cold. Oo! Ah! I can see a town. It is called (*local town*). Ahh!

Vileun What can you see?

Astra Nothing. It is half-day closing. Oo! I pass on! On! I now see a small village. It is called . . . Merry . . . Merrydale! Oo! I can see an old man in a house with a white beard . . . the old man has the beard not the house. Oo! Ahhh!

Vileun What is it?

Astra It is *He*! It is the one you seek. It is Santa Claus!

Vileun Ah! Tell me more!

Astra (*staggering about*) Ooo! My powers grow weak . . . The picture is fading . . . it is gone! (*She comes out of the trance*) Oh, I'm sure I've damaged my astral plane!

Vileun So! We know that Santa Claus is to be found in a village called Merrydale. Christmas is in the Earth month of December. What month is it on Earth now? Quick! Tell me!

Astra Well, er . . . let me think. Mars is over Venus . . . Jupiter's up there (*pointing up*) and Uranus is down there. (*Pointing down*)

Vileun What!

Astra Neptune's going down for the third time . . . Saturn's on the slide . . . er . . . take away the first planet you 'thought of . . . (*counting on her fingers*) . . . er . . . December! (*To Vileun, in triumph*) The present Earth month *is* December!

Vileun Ah!

Astra And with only (*number*) shopping days left . . . it must be Christmas *next week*!

Vileun Then there is no time to be lost! Santa Claus must be taken at once! Summon my astronauts! I leave for Earth this instant!

Astra picks up the book etc. and exits

Ha! Ha! Ha! Great glistening globs of gamma gore! I shall soon have Santa Claus and the planet Earth will be in my power like all the rest!

Null and Void enter

Ah! My astronauts! Prepare my fastest space craft. We leave for Earth immediately!

Null (*puzzled*) Earth?

Vileun That's what I said!

Null Never heard of it. Have you, Void?

Void (*dumbly*) No, Null.

Vileun To the launching pads! (*He pushes Null towards exit*) Look alive! Look alive! (*To Void*) And you—do the best you can!

Vileun pushes Null and Void off stage

Vileun (*following*) If the miserable inhabitants of Earth do not accept me as their Lord and Master they will never see Santa Claus again! Ha! Ha! Away! Destination—Earth! Ha! Ha! Ha!

Vileun exits

The Lights fade to a Black-out

SCENE 2

The Village of Merrydale, Earth

Full set. A "Dickensian" Christmas card scene. Dame Dangle's cottage on stage right. Santa's house on stage left. Both have practical front doors. Over Santa's door hangs a sign which reads, "Professor Atnas—High Class Inventor".

In the background are snow laden cottages and trees

The Villagers and Village children are discovered singing and dancing

Song 1 (*Tommy, Village Children and Villagers*)

After the song, the 1st Girl shows her rag doll to the other girls

1st Girl Look at my new dolly.

The girls gather around to have a look. Little Tommy Tucker creeps up, and grabs the doll. He runs to the boys and they start throwing it to each other, just out of the 1st Girl's reach. She jumps up and down yelling and screaming. The other girls cry out in protest

(*Yelling and trying to retrieve her doll*) My dolly! Give me back my dolly! Give it to me!

At last she gets hold of it only to find Tommy Tucker grasping one arm of the doll. There is a tug of war. The boys shout for Tommy. The girls still yell in protest. Tommy suddenly lets go of the doll and the 1st Girl falls over. Tommy and the boys roar with laughter. The girls help the 1st Girl to her feet. She discovers her doll is broken and lets out a long, high pitched wail. The others cringe at the sound

Villager 1 Coo! What a noise!
Villager 2 (*to girls*) Can't you shut her up!
Villager 3 We'll have the Fire Brigade here in a minute!
2nd Girl It's *your* fault, Tommy Tucker! You broke the doll!
Tommy No, I didn't!
Girls Oh, yes, you did!
Boys Oh, no, he didn't!

This continues for a while until Villager 1 notices that the 1st Girl has stopped wailing

Villager 1 (*to others*) Hey! She's stopped!

They all sigh with relief. A slight pause then the 1st Girl starts wailing again. All go back to shouting at each other

     Dame Dangle rushes from her cottage

Dame (*shouting over the din*) Oy! What's goin' on? I won't have it, whatever it is! (*She parts the boys from the girls*) Break! End of round! Oh! That's a foul! Ref, send him off! *Be quiet!*

Everyone goes silent but Dame Dangle continues to yell

     Bee Quiiiiet! (*She notices she is the only one making a noise and feels very foolish*) Oo! That's made me go all of a do da! (*Seeing the audience*) Oh, look! We've got company! (*To the audience*) Hello, you lot!

There are a few replies

     It must be Sunday! Come on, give yer tonsils a treat! When I shout— Hello, you lot—I want *you* to shout back—Hello, Dame Dangle! Here goes! Hello you lot!

The audience shouts back

     That's better! Let's try something else! HI DE HI!

The audience shouts back

     And another one! UMPAH! UMPAH!
Children (*yelling at her*) Stick it up your jumpah!
Dame (*to Children*) I wasn't talkin' to *you*, you loud lot of lousy little layabouts, you! Why were you making all that din just now? The noise was enough to wake the dead!

Tommy Sorry, we didn't know you were sleeping!

They all laugh

Dame (*grabbing him by the ear*) And that's quite enough from you, Little Tommy Tucker. (*To the audience*) Oh, he's a right little horror, this one. A real juvenile detergent! Anyone want to take him home with them? You could hang him on your front door to frighten off salesmen! (*To Tommy*) I don't want any more lip from you. I haven't forgot what you said about me yesterday!

Villager 1 What did he say?

Dame I'm not tellin'.

All Oh, go on!

Dame Shan't!

3rd Girl You tell us, Tommy.

Tommy I . . .

Dame (*rolling up her sleeves*) Just you dare!

Tommy I . . . All right. I won't tell.

Dame Promise?

Tommy Yes. And I'm very sorry for what I said.

Dame (*patting him on the head*) There's a dear little chap.

Tommy I don't *really* think you look like King Kong—*he's* not so hairy!

Everyone roars with laughter as Dame Dangle chases Tommy around

Dame Oo! You little . . . You wait . . . I'll . . . (*She stops chasing, out of puff*) No, I'll not demean meself chasing after him! (*To the audience*) To tell you the truth, girls, I can hardly move. It's this new girdle I've got on. Oh! It gives me terrible twinges in me twin set. There's no room for extension, you see. Talk about cross your heart, it's more like cross your fingers and hope for the best! Do you know the feeling?

Audience participation

(*To children*) Now then, you lot, you still haven't told me what all that rumpus was about.

The Villagers begin to drift off

All the children try to explain at once. The 1st Girl starts her high pitched wail again

One at a time! Shut yer cake holes!

All stop except the 1st Girl who continues to wail. The Dame does a "double take". Comic business with Dame putting her hand over the girl's mouth and taking it away, making the wail sound like a Red Indian war cry. This she does until the girl runs out of breath and stops

(*To 1st Girl*) Have you done? What's the matter, dear? You sounded like (*pop singer*) with his throat cut.

The 1st Girl explains in a series of wails, sobs, gurgles and sniffs

(*Dumbfounded*) Yes, well . . . don't pick it, and it'll soon get better.

1st Girl (*pointing to Tommy*) He broke my dolly!

Dame (*taking the doll and rounding on Tommy*) Is this true? Did you broll her dakey, I mean . . . drake her brolly . . . I mean . . . did you do *this*? (*She holds up the doll*)

Tommy No!

Dame I bet you did! (*To the audience*) He did, didn't he?

Audience participation

(*To 1st Girl*) Never mind, my little sugar plum. Nice Dame Dangle will repair your dolly for you. I'm good at fixin' things that's busted.

Tommy Why don't you do something about your face then?

The children laugh

Dame Oh, go and hire yourself out as a dartboard, you! (*Taking hold of the doll*) Now, let's see. Ah, yes! If I push this bit here . . . and pull that bit there . . . (*She pulls and the doll's other arm comes off*) Oh! (*She holds up both arms and giggles foolishly*) Now it's quite 'armless.

The 1st Girl starts wailing again. Dame Dangle tries to quieten her. Finally, out of desperation, she stuffs the doll into the girl's mouth, where it hangs

(*Rounding on Tommy again*) This is all your fault, Tommy Tucker!

5th Girl (*to Tommy*) Yes! You'd better repair her doll, or I'm going to tell her father *you* broke it!

Dame So there! (*She takes the doll from the girl's mouth, and plants it into Tommy's hands*) Get fixin'!

Tommy No! (*He throws the doll back to Dame*) I don't know anything about stupid dolls!

5th Girl (*taking the doll and giving it to the 1st Girl*) Come on, let's go and tell your father what he did!

Dame (*to Tommy, rubbing her hands in glee*) Yes! And I hope he gives you a *welt* with his *belt* where it's *felt*!

5th Girl (*putting her arm around the 1st Girl*) Come on.

The Girls turn to go

Tommy Wait! *I* can't fix it, but I know someone who can.

All Who?

Tommy Professor Atnas! He's an inventor, isn't he? He's bound to be able to repair a silly old doll.

Dame Go on then, Mr Know-all-knickers! There's his house! (*She points to Santa's house*) Go and ask him!

They all move to Santa's house. Tommy knocks on the door and it swings open

Tommy It's open! (*He calls inside*) Hello! . . . Professor Atnas! . . . Are you at home? . . . (*Nothing. He turns to the others*) He must be out.

2nd Boy He might be in the laboratory.

Dame (*shocked*) Oh! You rude little boy! (*Great dawning*) Oh, the *laboratory* . . . I thought you said . . . er . . . (*To Tommy*) Go in and have a look!

Tommy (*nervously*) What, in there?

All Yes!

Tommy But . . . But I've never been in his house. It looks all dark and creepy!

Dame Oh, is little Mr Mighty Mouth scared?

Tommy (*moving away*) Ju . . . Just a bit.

Dame Well, you know what to do, don't you?

Tommy What?

Dame Whistle!

Children Whistle?

Dame Yes! It always helps!

Song 2 (*Dame with Village Children*)

After the song, Dame Dangle pushes Tommy towards Santa's house

Dame Off you go, Superman! Into the dark inferior!

Tommy (*at the doorway, looking in*) It . . . it looks spooky . . . I'll go tomorrow!

Tommy moves away quickly but Dame Dangle grabs him

Dame Oo! You little cowardy custard, you! *I* wouldn't be afraid!

Tommy You *go* then!

Dame Me?

Children Yes!

Dame (*getting the shakes*) I . . . I'm much too busy . . . yes . . . I've got washing to put in the oven, and a cake to hang out!

Dame Dangle makes a dash for her cottage but the children stop her and push her towards Santa's house

Oh! Don't push! Mind me odds and ends! Oh! (*At the doorway she looks in, very scared*) Oo! It *does* look creepy! (*To children*) You don't really want me to go in there, do you?

Children Yes!

Dame (*to the audience*) Shall I?

Audience participation

(*Trying to be brave*) Oh, well! Into the great behind . . . I mean, beyond! Here goes!

Dame Dangle creeps into the house

There is a loud crash from inside

(*Off*) Oo! It's so dark in here! I can't see me face in front me hands! Ah! What's that? . . . Ooo! Ah!

There is a loud bang, followed by a flash

The Villagers rush on

Dame Dangle runs, screaming, from the house. She cowers on the other side of stage

Ooo! It was 'orrible! 'Orrible!

All What?

Dame A m . . . m . . . monster! Ten feet tall! Oo!

Roberta the Robot appears in the doorway of Santa's house

Roberta Beep! Beep!

Dame Ah! It's the monster! Oh! Someone save me!

Roberta comes out and shakes hands with the awestruck children and villagers

Roberta Hello! Nice to meet you. Beep! Nice to meet you. Beep! Nice to meet you. Beep!

Villager It's a robot!

Roberta My name is Roberta. I am the invention of Professor Atnas. Beep! (*She bows then moves towards Dame Dangle*) Hello. Nice to meet you. Beep! (*She holds out her hand to Dame Dangle*)

Dame (*cringing*) Oh! It's going to excruciate me!

3rd Boy It only wants to be friendly, Dame Dangle.

Dame I don't care if it's got a cheque from Littlewoods! Keep it away from me!

Roberta (*moving nearer to Dame Dangle*) Beep! Beep?

Dame Oh, go and beep somewhere else, you demented dustbin, you!

Roberta moves to centre where they all gather around her. Dame Dangle keeps at a safe distance

4th Boy Isn't it good!

2nd Girl What did it say its name was?

Roberta My name is Roberta. I am the invention of Professor Atnas. Beep! (*She bows*)

Villager What sort of things can you do, Roberta?

Roberta I have been programmed to do anything. Beep!

Children Coo!

Villager Can you sing?

Roberta Affirmative! (*She sings a short snatch from a current pop song*)

5th Boy Can you tell jokes?

Roberta Affirmative!

Roberta does a "Knock knock" joke with the children and they roar with laughter

6th Boy Can you do impressions?

Roberta Affirmative! (*She does an impresion of a well known TV personality*)

They all laugh and clap

What is your next command?

6th Girl Show Dame Dangle that you want to be friends with her.

Roberta Affirmative! Beep! (*She moves to Dame Dangle*)

Dame (*cowering away*) Oo! Don't let it near *me*! I don't want to catch metal fatigue!

Roberta opens a panel on her chest

Dame Ah! It's goin' to show me its infernal workings!

Roberta takes out a flower and holds it up to Dame Dangle

Roberta So pleased to make your acquaintance. Beep!

Dame (*all fright disappearing at the sight of the flower*) Well! I'll go to the foot of our compost heap! A flow-flow for me! Oh, how sweet! (*She takes the flower and sniffs it*) Oh, essence of sump oil! (*To the audience*) She's not a bad little tin can after all, is she?

Roberta Beep! Hic! Beep! Hic!

Dame Sounds like you've got dirt on your distributeutor! Well, thank you very much, Roberta. Is there anything I can get *you*? A nice bag of mixed nuts and bolts, perhaps—or how about a pint of four star?

Roberta starts beeping loudly and spins around on the spot. She stops spinning, and her arms wave about uncontrollably. She gives one long "running down" beep and doubles over. She remains like this, giving little spasmodic jerks

All (*clustering round Roberta*) Roberta! What's happened? What's the matter with her? etc.

Dame (*pushing her way in*) Oh, lor! What's up with her? Oo! Look! I think her big end's gone! Crikey! What'll Professor Atnas say? He'll think we've deaded her! Oh, what are we going to do?

Villager Let's try to get her back into the house.

They start to move Roberta

Tommy (*looking off and pointing*) Too late! Here comes Professor Atnas!

Everyone rushes upstage, leaving Dame Dangle alone with the defunct Roberta. She panics and just manages to cover the robot with her skirts

> *Santa Claus, alias Professor Atnas, enters. His disguise consists of a green jacket, a velvet smoking cap, a bright yellow waistcoat, and loud check trousers. He wears gold spectacles and a short white apron. No attempt has been made to conceal his flowing white hair and beard*

Santa (*waving to everyone*) Good morning, everyone!

All (*waving back*) Good morning, Professor.

Santa (*moving down*) And a good morning to you, Dame Dangle.

Dame Good mor ... Ah!

Roberta gives a jerk and sends the Dame crashing into Santa

(*Flustered, but trying to smile sweetly*) Good morning, air pressure ... I mean, Professor! (*She backs away with difficulty, pushing Roberta back as she does so*)

Santa (*looking out front*) Isn't it a wonderful morning?

Dame (*being jerked about by Roberta*) Yes! ... Oh! ... Smashin' ... Oh! ... Ah! ...

Santa is watching Dame Dangle very puzzled. She tries to turn the jerks into a dance with her skirts held out

Ha! Ha! Makes you want to dance and sing, doesn't it? Tra la la! "Oh, what a beautiful mornin' ..."

Santa (*looking out front again*) I've just had a marvellous constitutional.

Dame Good! That All-Bran's great stuff, isn't it? (*Aside to Roberta*) Give over, you gyrating junk pile!

Santa (*still looking front*) There's nothing like it! A good bracing walk across the hills, with the wind blowing in your face!

Roberta emits a very loud noise. Santa looks at Dame Dangle. Dame Dangle smiles sweetly, and taps her chest

Dame Oh, manners! Yes, there's a lot of wind about this morning!

Roberta starts making strange noises and jerks about uncontrollably. Dame Dangle attempts to hide her but gets knocked to the ground for her pains

Santa (*seeing Roberta and rushing over*) Roberta! What are you doing out here? What's the matter with you? (*To Dame Dangle*) What have you done to my robot?

Dame (*crawling to her feet*) I ... we ... Oh, heck! Excuse me, I think me dumplings are boilin' over!

Dame Dangle runs into her cottage

Santa examines Roberta. The others move down

Villager We didn't do anything, Professor. It just happened.

Santa I see. Well, I know what the trouble is. Her cogitater keeps sticking. I really *must* get that perfected. Otherwise she's a splendid invention ... er ... don't you agree?

All Oh, yes!

Santa She'll be a terrific help to me next week, when I deliver all those presents ... Oh! ... Ah! (*He coughs, realizing he has said too much. Quickly he takes a screwdriver from his apron pocket and turns to Roberta*) Now let me see—(*He mades some adjustments to Roberta's control panel*) There! That should do the trick!

Roberta springs back to life

Roberta Beep! Beep! Hello master!

Santa Hello, Roberta. (*To the others*) Now, would you like to see Roberta do something *really* special?

All Yes, please!

Santa (*to the audience*) Would *you*?

Audience participation

Very well! Roberta, your dance number if you please.

Roberta Affirmative! A beep! A beep! A beep, beep beep!

Song 3 (*Roberta's Dance*)

After the dance, everyone claps and cheers. Roberta takes a bow, then spins around and doubles over as before

Santa Oh, dear! It's happened again. I shall have to take her into the laboratory. (*He picks up Roberta or pushes her towards his house*) Goodbye, everyone.
All Goodbye, Professor.

Santa exits with Roberta

The Villagers exit

As soon as the stage is clear of adults, the children gather excitedly around Tommy

2nd Boy What do you think he meant when he said he had all those presents to deliver next week?
Children It's Christmas next week!
Tommy There's only one person I know with a fat belly, a white beard and lots of presents to deliver at Christmas time!
Children *Santa Claus!*
Tommy Yes! I wonder!

Dame Dangle rushes on from her cottage, in great excitement

Dame Kids! Kids! Oh, I've just had a wonderful surprise!
3rd Boy You're going to have a facelift at last!
Dame You'll never guess who's come to spend Christmas with me!
2nd Girl Dracula?
Dame No! It's me nephew! Dick! Captain Dick Daring of the Royal Foot and Mouth! (*She marches to one side, and shouts in Sergeant Major fashion*) Company! Form a line!

The children get into a straight line

Attention!

The children snap to attention

About turn!

The children turn upstage

Quick ...

One of the children starts to move

Wait for it! Wait for it! Quick March!

The children march upstage

Halt!

The children halt, in line with Dame Dangle's cottage door

Face front!

The children do so

Eyes right!

The children turn their heads to the cottage door

Captain Dick Daring enters from the cottage and salutes

Dame Dangle and the children salute

Dick (*laughing and moving down*) At ease, men!

Dame (*bringing Dick to* C) Let's have a proper look at you, nephew. Oh! Doesn't he look swish? All that gilt and gingerbread! (*Tweaking Dick's cheek*) Oh, you handsome hunk of he-man, you! (*To the audience*) Don't you think he's the cat's whiskers, eh? He makes Burt Reynolds look like Sid Little! You can see which side of the family he takes after, can't you? (*She preens herself*) Oh, yes! The family resonance is unmistakable!

Tommy (*to Dame Dangle*) He doesn't look a bit like you! You're *fat*!

Dame I . . . I'm *not* fat! I've just got a small head, that's all. Anyway, who asked you to poke your nose in, farmyard features? (*She pushes Tommy away, then turns to Dick*) How long can you stay, Dick?

Dick Only until Boxing Day, I'm afraid, Aunty. Then I must return to my regiment.

Dame Don't you get fed up with being a soldier? All that pit and spolish and marchin' about.

Dick It's a grand life, Aunty!

Song 4 (*Dick with Dame and Children*)

As the number ends the children exit, saluting Dick as they go

Dame What does a Captain have to do?

Dick Well, I have to inspect the arms . . .

Dame Oh, so do I. The Butcher's Arms . . . The King's Arms . . .

Dick And make sure they're well oiled.

Dame Oh, yes! Especially on Saturday nights!

Dick Then, I have to keep a close watch on the Privates.

Dame Er . . . yes! . . . er . . . Oh! Look at the medals! (*To the audience*) He's got a chest like (*local jeweller's*) window! (*Pointing to a medal*) What's that one for?

Dick That's for valour in the field.

Dame Oh, I should have one of them! I used to have lots of valour when the young lads took me to the field! (*She points to the next medal*) What's this one for?

Dick That's a campaign medal.

Dame I've got one of them on me bed.

Dick A medal?

Dame No, a Counterpane! (*She points to the next medal*) And this one?

Dick That's a Coronation Medal.

Dame Oh, do you get medals for watching that? I watch it every week. I just love that little Mavis Riley, don't you?

Crystal enters, looking about her as if lost. She does not see the others

Dame (*nudging Dick*) 'Ere! Who dat?

Dick (*aside to Dame Dangle*) I don't know, Aunty, but I'll soon find out. (*He crosses to Crystal*) Good morning, Miss.

Crystal (*turning, startled*) Oh! . . . Good morning.

Dick Daring is the name, Miss. Captain Dick Daring. (*He salutes*) You seem lost. Can I be of any assistance?

Dame Dangle moves behind Dick and crouches, listening hard

Crystal Thank you, Captain. I am looking for the house of Professor Atnas.

Dick Well I'm a stranger here myself but I'm sure my Aunt can help you. Aunty? (*He turns and bumps into Dame Dangle*)

Dame Oh! Steady on, nephew! I got your DSO right in me YMCA. (*To Crystal, pointing*) That's the Professor's house, over there.

Crystal Thank you. (*She crosses to Santa's house, is about to knock, but she turns back to look at Dick*) Thank you, Captain Daring.

Dick (*moving to her*) Oh, *you* can call me Dick.

They gaze at each other

Dame (*to the audience*) Looks like he's on manoeuvres! (*Going up and taking Dick's arm*) Come on, soldier boy. It's *me* you've come to visit. Stop swashin' yer buckles and let's have a cup o' tea! (*She pulls Dick to her cottage*)

Dame Dangle exits, leaving the cottage door open

Dick lingers, unable to take his eyes of Crystal

Dame Dangle's arm appears and pulls Dick off into the cottage

Crystal knocks on Santa's door

Roberta answers the door

Roberta Not today, thank you. Beep! (*She is about to close the door*)

Crystal But ...

Santa (*off*) Who is it, Roberta?

Santa appears and comes out of his house. He is greatly surprised at seeing Crystal

Good gracious! Crystal! (*He brings her downstage, very secretively*) What are you doing here?

Crystal I'm afraid there's been some trouble, Santa.

Santa Shh! Not so loud. (*He looks around to make sure they are alone*) Now, what ...

Roberta (*pushing in between them*) My name is Roberta. Beep!

Santa Oh, Crystal, meet Roberta.

Roberta (*holding out hand to Crystal*) Hello. Nice to meet you. Beep!

Crystal (*shaking hands*) Nice to meet *you*, Roberta.

Santa (*aiming Roberta towards his house*) Now, run along, Roberta. Don't overtax your terminals.

Roberta is pushed into the house by Santa who closes the door after her

(*Returning to Crystal*) Now then, you spoke of trouble.

Crystal It's the elves.

Santa Oh, dear! Not again! It's the same every year! What's the matter with them this time?

Crystal Well, the *red* elves say it's *their* job to put eyes on the Teddy Bears and the *green* elves say it's *their* job. Consequently, nothing has been done. There's piles and piles of Teddy Bears with no eyes! I've tried talking to the elves but they won't listen to anyone but you. I'm afraid you'll have to come back to the factory at once if there's going to be any Teddies this Christmas.

Santa Oh dear, oh dear, oh dear! . . . Well, I suppose I shall have to. Really, those elves are the limit! I'll just collect my things, Crystal, and we'll leave at once.

Santa exits to his cottage, muttering about the elves

Dick enters from Dame Dangle's cottage

Dick Ah! Nice to meet you again, Miss . . . er . . .

Crystal (*moving downstage*) My name is Crystal.

Dick (*moving to her*) Crystal. How charming. It's such a . . . such a *clear* name, isn't it?

Tommy and the Village children enter at the back

Crystal, I . . . I was wondering—as we're both strangers here, couldn't we explore the village together?

Crystal I'm very sorry, Captain, but Professor Atnas and I must leave here at once.

The children react at this

Dick Leave at once! But why?

Crystal Oh, . . . er . . . a personal matter. (*She moves up to Santa's door*)

Dick (*following*) And when will you be returning to Merrydale?

Crystal I'm afraid we shall never return. Goodbye.

Crystal exits

Dick moves down stage, crestfallen. The children move down, very excited

Tommy (*to others*) He's leaving Merrydale. That *proves* it's him.

Children Yes!

Dick (*turning*) Hello! What's all the excitement?

Tommy (*to others*) Shall I tell him?

The children nod

(*To Dick*) Promise you won't laugh?

Dick You have my word as an officer and a gentleman.

Tommy (*moving to Dick, very confidentially*) We think that Professor Atnas is really—Santa Claus.

Dick Santa . . . (*He is about to laugh then remembers his oath*) But, doesn't Santa Claus live at the North Pole? What would he be doing in Merrydale?

3rd Girl We don't know *that*, but we're sure he's Santa.

Dick Why?

4th Boy Earlier, he made a slip about having lots of presents to deliver next week.

Dick So what?

4th Boy (*darkly*) Then there's his *name*.

5th Boy Yes! (*He points to the sign over Santa's door*) Look!

Dick goes upstage and looks at the sign. The children join him

Dick (*reading*) "Professor Atnas. High Class Inventor." (*To children*) What's strange about that?

6th Boy Spell it backwards, Captain.

Dick (*puzzled*) Backwards?

Children Yes! Go on!

Dick (*looking at sign*) Atnas ... S A N T A ... Santa ... it spells Santa!

Children See!

Tommy Now he's leaving the village. That means he's going back to the North Pole to get ready for Christmas next week!

Dick (*moving down*) You know, my young friends, I think you're right. There's only one way to find out for sure.

Children (*moving down to him*) How?

Dick We must take him by surprise! Catch him off guard. Here's how we'll do it!

The children gather round

When he comes out, we'll all shout, "Oh Santa!" If he answers, we'll know it's him.

Children Yes!

Dick (*to the audience*) You'll help us, won't you?

Audience participation

Good! Now, remember, you have to shout—"Oh, Santa!" when I give the sign and not before.

6th Boy (*pointing to Santa's door*) Look out! He's coming!

Dick and the children move to the right-hand side of stage

Santa enters from his house, followed by Crystal and Roberta

Sants wears a long overcoat, a top hat and a long, woollen scarf. He carries a carpet bag

Santa (*surprised at seeing the children*) Oh! ... er ... Hello, children.

Children Hello, Professor!

Santa (*aside to Crystal*) Oh, dear! This could be difficult! (*To children, lost for words*) I ... I'm afraid I have to leave Merrydale ... at once ... er ... something has come up ... yes ... well ... goodbye!

Santa, Crystal and Roberta, start to exit. Dick quickly gives a sign to the children and audience

Dick
Children } (*together*) Oh, Santa!

Santa (*turning, absently*) Yes? ... Oh! (*He realizes he's been caught out*)
Crystal (*aside to Santa*) They know! (*She takes the carpet bag*)
Santa (*coming down*) It would appear so. (*To children*) Well, it seems you have discovered my secret. Yes, I am Santa Claus.

All the children rush at him, glibbering with excitement

(*Quietening them, gently*) Shh! Shh! Now that you know the truth, you must promise not to tell anyone.
Children We promise!
Santa (*to the audience*) That goes for you as well! Promise?

Audience participation

Tommy But what are you doing in Merrydale, Santa? We all thought you lived at the North Pole.
Santa Oh, I haven't done for years, my boy. I used to, when I was younger, but now that I'm getting on a bit I can't stand the cold. All that snow and ice ... Brrr! So throughout the year I live in different parts of the world, under disguise of course. My factory is still at the Pole but I only return to it on December the twenty-third when it's time to collect the toys for my deliveries on Christmas Eve.
5th Girl But I always send my letters to you at the North Pole.
Santa And quite right, my dear. That's where my assistant, Crystal, comes in. She receives all your letters and forwards them on to wherever I'm staying.
6th Girl Just think, we had Santa Claus living in our own village and didn't know it.
Santa And that's how I want it to stay, my dears. All that I have told you must remain a closely guarded secret.

Dame Dangle enters from her cottage; at the same time the Villagers drift on

Dick (*to Santa*) Fear not, your secret is safe with us!
Dame (*pushing in*) Secret! What secret?
Dick Oh, ... er ... nothing, Aunty.
Dame Come on!
Dick I can't tell you!
Dame Oh, go on! The suspenders is killing me! (*To the children*) You tell me!
Children No!
Dame (*stamping her feet*) Tell me, tell me, tell me!!
Children (*copying her*) No, no, no!!
Dame Oh, you mean lot! It isn't fair, leaving me out! (*To the audience*) You'll tell me, won't you? What's the secret? What is it? Tell me!

The others signal to the audience to say "no"

Dame Oo! You rotten lot! (*She starts to blubber*) It's not fair! (*She goes to one side, wailing like a spoilt brat*)
Santa (*to the audience*) Oh dear. I'd better tell her or she'll flood us out in a minute. (*He crosses to Dame Dangle*) Dame Dangle?

Dame Dangle tosses her head

Dame Dangle, I've decided to tell you the secret.

Dame (*turning, all tears gone*) I should think so an' all!

Santa But you must promise not to tell anyone else.

Dame Oh, you know me, the soul of description! (*Cupping her ear*) Gi' me! Gi' me!

Santa I am Santa Claus.

Dame You are ... (*She roars with laughter*) Ha! Ha! Oh, pull the other one, it's got Jingle Bells on! Santa Claus indeed! Ha! Ha! If he's Santa Claus then I'm Bo Derek! Ha! Ha! Ha!

Santa takes his red coat from the carpet bag and holds it up

Santa Dame Dangle ... look!

Dame (*looking*) A red coat! So what! I've got blue knickers on but I ain't Maggie Thatcher!

Santa gives the coat to Crystal, who returns it to the bag

Santa I can prove to you that I am Santa Claus.

Dame '*Ow*, may I be so bold as to hask?

Santa I'll tell you what I brought you last Christmas. (*He whispers in Dame Dangle's ear*) Am I right?

Dame Yes! And you could have brought me a pair that fitted! (*Suddenly struck*) He ... he *is* Santa! Oh, buckle me brooms and dent me dustpan! Oo! Santa! Let me give you a kiss! (*She does so*) Cor! It's like kissin' a Brillo pad! 'Ere, Santa, there's something I've always wanted to know.

Santa What's that?

Dame Do you sleep with it under or over the sheets?

Santa I beg your pardon!

Dame (*pointing to his beard*) This! The face fungus!

Santa Oh, I see. Under in winter and over in the summer.

Dame That's what I thought.But what are you doing in Merrydale, Santa?

Crystal That's a long story and I'm afraid Santa and I must leave at once.

Santa Yes, I have some trouble with my elves.

Dame Oh, you want to try TCP, that always works on me! But you can't leave just like that, Santa! You've got to have a proper send off! (*To the others*) Hasn't he?

All Yes!

Dame We must have a party!

All Oh, yes!

Santa But ...

Dame Don't worry, it'll be a secret party. Just us lot. We'll have it at your place, cos you've got a bigger chamber! You can put on yer proper Santa clobber! I'll go down to the shops and get some cakes! What do you say, Sant?

Santa Well, I ...

Children Oh, please!

Santa (*after a look at their eager faces*) Oh, very well!

All Hurray!

Santa But it must only be a *short* party.
Dame It'll be the shortest party since the SDP!

Song 5 (*All*)

The number ends with a dance, during which Santa and the Villagers dance off into his house. Dick and Crystal, dancing together, follow. Dame Dangle and Roberta finish with a comic dance then Dame Dangle exits into her cottage and Roberta into Santa's house

A slight pause, then strange noises are heard, getting louder and louder. The stage gradually grows dark. A Flying Saucer descends and lands with flashing lights and smoke

Null and Void emerge from the saucer, followed by Vileun, the Vile

Vileun Well, here we are on the planet Earth! In the village of Merrydale! Now to find Santa Claus! Ha! Ha! Ha! (*He laughs his terrible laugh*)

The Lights fade to a Black-out

SCENE 3

Another part of the village

Tabs, or a front cloth showing the village street with shops and houses decorated for Christmas

Vileun enters, followed by the reluctant Null and Void

Vileun (*pulling them to C*) Come on! Come on! Now, I want you to search for Santa Claus. He's a fat old fool with a white beard. Go on! Get searching! (*He pushes them towards exit*) Go on! Move!

Null and Void exit

(*To the audience*) Ha! Ha! Ha! Very soon now, I, Vileun the Vile, will be master of this miserable planet Earth! Oh, yes I will!

Audience participation

Once I have found Santa Claus, and taken him prisoner, all you nasty little Earthlings will be in my power! The choice will be yours. If you still want Santa at Christmas you will have to accept *me* as your supreme ruler! If you refuse you will never see the old fool again! Ha! Ha!

Null and Void enter

(*Rushing to Null*) Well! Have you found him? Have you found Santa Claus?
Null (*shaking his head*) No.
Vileun (*to Void*) What about you? Have you found Santa Claus's whereabouts?
Void (*dumbly*) What colour are they?

Vileun Ah! You lunar lumps! Listen, he must be found at once! He is somewhere here, in this village. Astra, the astrologer, saw him in one of her trances—and she was adamant!

Void Adam Ant? She looks more like (*pop star*)

Vileun Find me Santa Claus, or—it's the disintegrating ray for you both!

Vileun takes out a ray gun which he points at Null and Void, who cringe away

Now make a thorough search this time! (*Pointing left*) I will take this side of the village. (*Pointing right*) You take that. (*To the audience*) Ha! Ha! Santa Claus will be soon be my prisoner! Ha! Ha! Ha!

Vileun exits, laughing

As soon as he is gone, Void starts to exit, copying Vileun's laughter and movements

Void (*a bad copy*) Har! Har! Har!

Null Oy! Darth Vader! Where are you going?

Void (*as Vileun*) I'm going to find Santa Claus! Har! Har! Har! (*He starts to go*)

Null (*pulling him back*) Come here, you galactic goon! Just ask yourself this. Why are we here? Go on, ask yourself that!

Void (*very puzzled, taking a step right and looking left*) Why are we here? (*Stepping left, looking right*) *I* don't know. Why *are* we here? (*Stepping right, looking left*) I asked *you* first! (*Stepping left, looking right*) Oh, no you didn't! (*Stepping right, looking left*) Oh, yes I did! (*This continues, getting faster and faster*)

Null (*grabbing him*) Stop it! Stop it!

Void Well, you asked me to ask me!

Null Listen, why should we help kidnap this Santa Claus? He sounds like a nice old chap to me. Giving away toys and presents every year.

Void What's this Christmas thing like?

Null I don't know. It sounds like a lot of fun. We'll have to ask the Earthlings. I think there's some out there. (*He points to the audience*)

Void What, *live* ones?

Null Well, I'm not sure about that. (*Going forward and calling to the audience*) Hello! Earth people! Are you receiving me? Are you out there?

Audience participation

Null (*to Void*) They're out there.

Void is terrified. He runs upstage and cowers with his back to the audience. His knees are shaking and he covers his eyes

Null What's the matter?

Void I'm sacred! We don't know what the Earth creatures are like! They might be hid ... hideous monsters!

Null (*gulping and moving back*) I ... I never thought of that! (*To the audience very nervously*) Are you hideous monsters?

Audience participation

Void They sound pretty hideous, don't they?

Null There's only one way to find out. I'll light them up with my illuminating ray! (*He takes out a ray gun and points it at the audience*) Here goes!

The House Lights come up

(*Peering at the audience*) Cor! What a funny looking lot!

Void (*still covering his eyes*) Wh ... what are they like? Are they horrible?

Null Not really. They're a bit like us, only not as handsome. Come and have a look.

Void moves down, very slowly, and peers at the audience through his fingers. Suddenly he yells with fright

Void Ahh! You said they weren't horrible! Look at *that* one! (*He points*)

Null Now, don't get them angry. Let's try communicating with them.

Void No, let's try talking to them first.

Null (*to the audience*) Hello!

Audience participation

Knock! Knock!

Audience shout back to Void

They don't seem too bad, do they? You say something.

Void Er ... something!

Null (*to the audience*) What sort of things do you do at Christmas?

Audience participation ad lib. Null and Void bring conversation around to Christmas Carols

Carols? Carol's *what*? Oh, singing. I think they'd better come up here and show us!

Several children are invited on stage, and asked to sing a song

Song 6 (*Null and Void, with Audience*)

Null and Void give children sweets and take them back to their seats. They then return to the stage

The House Lights go down

Void (*with his head on Null's shoulder*) I fink I like Christmas, Null.

Null Same here, Void. We can't let old grizzle guts spoil it, can we? (*To audience*) If Vileun asks you about Santa Claus, don't tell him anything. He's a rotten old nasty!

Void I'd like to kick him right up the cosmos!

Vileun enters behind Null and Void. Audience participation in "He's behind you!" routine

Vileun Bah! Great lumps of lunar lava! I've searched that side of the village and found no trace of the wretched Santa Claus! (*To Null and Void*) Have *you* found him?

Null
Void } (*together*) { No!

Vileun Ah! You useless blockheads! I'd be better off with androids!

Void No, you wouldn't. They're painful!

Vileun Someone in this horrible hamlet knows his whereabouts! I'll ask these miserable Earthlings! (*To the audience*) You know where Santa Claus is, don't you?

Null and Void signal audience to say "No". "Oh, yes you do!" "Oh, no we don't!" routine follows

Bah! These are very low grade Earthlings! A mindless rabble! We must catch one on its own and extract the truth!

Void With or without gas?

Vileun What!

Void You said we were going to extract the tooth.

Vileun *Truth*, you space oddity, *truth*! Go and find me one single Earth creature so that I can pick its brains.

Null Ugh! You mucky pup!

Vileun (*roaring*) FIND ME AN EARTHLING!

Null and Void go to exit. They stop dead, looking off in terror. Void yells

What's the matter with you?

Null (*stammering and pointing off*) It's ... it's a monster!

Void And it's coming this way!

Vileun (*looking off*) What is it?

Null Is it a man?

Vileun Is it a bird?

Void Is it a plane?

   Dame Dangle skips on

Dame (*singing*) "Is it true what they say about Dixie? ..."

Vileun (*to others*) Ah! An Earthling! (*To the audience*) I *think*! (*He crosses to Dame Dangle*) Excuse me!

Dame Why, what have you done? (*Seeing Vileun's costume, to the audience*) Oo! Look at 'im! It's (*TV star or politician*)

Vileun Are you an Earthling?

Dame No, I'm with the Woolwich!

Vileun (*very deep*) Are you an inhabitant of the planet?

Dame (*to the audience*) Cor! Don't he talk funny? (*Mimicking Vileun's tone*) Mind your own business, fungus features!

Vileun How dare you address me that way!

Dame I haven't undressed you any way mate! That's wishful thinking on your part! (*To the audience*) What a cheek! (*To Vileun*) And stop pointing that beard at me, it might go off!

Vileun Be civil!

Dame (*coyly*) All right, I'll be *Sybil* if you'll be *Frank*!

Vileun Ah! You insufferable Earth woman!

Dame (*to Void*) 'Ere, who's he callin' a woman? (*She does a "double take" at the sight of Void's face. To Vileun*) Is *ET* with you?

Vileun I want something from you!

Dame Yes . . . well, you're not going to get it. Ta, ta! (*She starts to go*)

Vileun (*pushing her back*) *You* have information!

Dame Not any more. The doctor gave me something to rub in! (*She starts to go again*)

Vileun (*pushing her back*) I am seeking . . .

Dame Nice to meet you, Mr Seeking! (*She starts to go again*)

Vileun (*pushing her back*) I am seeking for someone. Someone I have travelled millions of light years to find!

Dame *Light* years! Oh, you want the (*Area Electricity Board*). (*She starts to go again*)

Vileun (*pushing her back*) I am Vileun the Vile, from the planet Varbos!

Dame Get away! You can't fool me! You're leftovers from (*well known local event*).

Vileun I shall soon be master of the entire Universe! Ha! Ha! Ha!

Dame (*to audience*) He's bonkers! I'm *off*!

Vileun (*grabbing her roughly*) Hold! Stay!

Dame (*pushing him off*) Oy! You hold your own stays, if you don't mind! (*She adjusts her clothes. To the audience*) What a sauce!!

Vileun (*very sinister*) Where can I find Santa Claus?

Dame Santa? Oh, that's easy! He's . . . (*To the audience*) No, I mustn't tell. I promised, didn't I? (*To Vileun*) Santa Claus? Never heard of him!

Vileun Out with it!

Dame Oh! Don't be rude!

Vileun Tell me where he is or I'll put you under hypnosis!

Dame You can put me under the sink for all I care!

Vileun (*to Null and Void*) Seize her!

Dame (*as they take hold of her*) Oo! Help! I've been grabbed by the aliens!

Vileun (*pushing his face close to hers*) Look into my eyes!

Dame No, thanks! I've got a weak tummy!

Vileun Look into my eyes! What do you see?

Dame Two lightly poached eggs!

Vileun (*in deep, hypnotic voice*) Soon you will be feeling sleepy . . . sleepy . . . sleepy . . .

Void falls asleep and snores loudly. Null prods him awake

(*to Dame Dangle, in the same voice*) Your eyelids grow heavy.

Dame (*copying his voice*) It's the way I'm built.

Vileun Sleep, sleep, deep deep, sleep.

Dame (*grabbing his hand*) Oh, shall we dance?

Dame Dangle twirls Vileun around, whistling the "Merry Widow" waltz. Null and Void start waltzing together. Vileun, with a roar, disentangles himself from Dame Dangle and pushes her back to Null and Void who take hold of her again

(*To the audience*) What a spoilsport! I was enjoyin' that!

Vileun Silence, Earth hag!

Dame (*to audience*) Oh, I shall give him such a thump in a minute!

Vileun pulls Dame close to him and stares deep into her eyes

Vileun By the powers of the Galaxy, most dread and chill, I command you,
O Earthling, succumb to my will!

*Dame Dangle immediately goes as rigid as a ramrod, her eyes wide open.
Vileun turns her to face front. She remains, standing bolt upright for a short
while, then slowly starts to lean sideways. Null and Void just manage to catch
her and set her upright again. Vileun passes his hand in front of her face a
couple of times*

Ha! Ha! She's under! Now to find the whereabouts of Santa Claus! (*Into
Dame's ear*) The only voice you hear is my voice. Whose voice do you
hear?

Dame (*baby talk*) Yours, daddy!

Vileun Do you know where I can find Santa Claus?

Dame (*as before*) Yeth, daddy.

Vileun Will you take me to him?

Dame Yeth, daddy.

Vileun Then lead on!

Dame Dangle exits in a sleepwalking fashion, arms out-stretched, etc.

(*To Null and Void*) Follow her! Don't let her out of your sight!

Null and Void exit in the same fashion

Santa Claus will soon be my prisoner! My plan for the domination of the
Universe is now complete! Ha! Ha! Ha!

Vileun exits

The Lights fade to a Black-out

Scene 4

A Room in Santa's House

*Full set. The classic inventor's den, part laboratory, workshop and study. Back
cloth and side wings show a cluttered array of workbenches, shelves, tools,
paint pots, diagrams, bits of inventions, book cases, etc., etc. There are
entrances right and left. Back centre stands a practical magic cabinet*

Dick and Crystal are discovered

Crystal I do wish your Aunt would hurry. Santa and I have a long journey
ahead of us.

Dick Oh, Crystal, I wish you didn't have to leave. Couldn't Santa manage
without you?

Crystal I am duty bound to be his assistant. Besides, I'm fond of him and would hate to hurt his feelings.

Dick You're not afraid of hurting mine!

Crystal (*as if she didn't know*) What do you mean?

Dick (*moving close to her*) You're leaving before I've had a chance to tell you how I feel about you. (*Taking her hands*) Oh, Crystal . . .

Song 7 (*Dick and Crystal*)

The Villagers and children rush on from the right, very excited

Tommy Here comes Santa!

All Hurry!

Santa and Roberta enter from the right. He now wears his red Santa Claus suit

Villager Three cheers for good old Santa! Hip hip!

All Hurray!

Villager Hip hip!

All Hurray!

Villager Hip hip!

All Hurray!

Santa (*beaming*) Thank you, my dears!

Tommy (*pointing to Santa's outfit*) Now he really *is* Santa Claus!

Santa (*dusting his sleeve*) It's a trifle shabby, I'm afraid. It's climbing down all those chimneys, you know. The soot plays havoc with it. (*To Crystal*) Is everything ready for the party? We haven't much time, you know.

Crystal We're waiting for Dame Dangle.

Dick She went to buy some cakes. I can't imagine what's keeping her.

Santa Well I hope she returns soon. We really must be going . . .

3rd Boy Santa? (*He points to the magic cabinet*) What's this?

Santa (*going to the cabinet*) Ah, that's part of my little hobby. This is my magic cabinet!

All Magic!

Santa Yes. Would you like to see some?

All Yes, please!

Santa (*to the audience*) Would you?

Audience participation

I thought perhaps you might. Now, let me see . . . Ah, yes! (*He goes to the 1st Girl*) May I borrow your doll for a short while, my dear?

1st Girl (*with a sob*) It's broken!

Santa I promise I'll repair it for you, in the twinkling of an eye. (*He takes the doll*) Thank you. (*To others*) May I present my charming assistant — Roberta!

Roberta wiggles about like a magician's assistant. All laugh and clap. Santa, in true magician style, hands the doll to Roberta. They both move to the cabinet

You see before you a completely empty cabinet. (*He throws open the door and knocks the sides of the cabinet*) I will ask my assistant to place the doll within.

Roberta, with a wiggle, puts the doll inside. Santa shuts the door

I will now utter the magic words and you will witness a marvellous magical mystery! (*He makes magic passes at cabinet*) HOCUS POCUS! Roberta, open the cabinet!

Roberta opens the door. A life size "doll" stands inside the cabinet. All are amazed. They clap

The "doll" steps from the cabinet and proceeds to dance

Song 8 (*Doll Dance*)

After the dance, the "doll" bows and everyone claps. The "doll" returns to the cabinet

1st Girl (*wailing*) That's not my dolly! He said he'd repair my dolly!
Santa And so I will, my dear. Roberta, close the door.

Roberta does so

And now, before your very eyes, I will return our dear little friend's doll, completely repaired! (*He makes magic passes at the cabinet*) HOCUS POCUS! Roberta, open the cabinet!

Roberta opens the door. The life size "doll" has vanished. Roberta takes the repaired doll out and hands it to Santa

(*Holding up the doll*) Behold! One doll as good as new! (*He hands the doll to the 1st Girl*)

All clap and cheer. Santa and Roberta take a bow. The 1st Girl runs to Santa and kisses him

1st Girl Oh, thank you, Santa! Thank you!
Villager (*pointing off, left*) Look! Here comes Dame Dangle!

Dame Dangle enters. She is still in a trance, arms out-stretched etc. Everyone reacts. She moves to the centre

Dick (*going to her*) Aunty! What's the matter?
Crystal What's wrong with her?
Santa I think she's been hypnotized!
Dame (*singing in childish voice*) "Ding dong bell, pussy's in the well . . ."
Dick Aunty!

Dick snaps his fingers in Dame's face. She leaps in the air with a yell

Dame (*running up and down*) Oh! I . . . how did I . . . what am I . . . where am I . . .? Ooo!
Dick (*taking her arm*) It's all right, Aunty. You're safe now.
Dame Oo! I don't half feel funny. I don't know if I'm on me head or me antimacassar! What happened?

Santa You were under the influence of hypnotism, Dame Dangle.
Dame Ger off! I haven't touched a single drop all day! (*To Dick*) What's he talkin' about? What's hip ... hip ... what he said, when it's at home?
Crystal Someone put you into a trance.
Dame A trance! Me? Fiddlefaddle! I'm not *trans*portable!
Dick Did you meet anyone when you went to get the cakes?
Dame No, I ... Oh! Those three funny lookin' men!
Dick What men?

Vileun enters from the left, following by Null and Void. All react

Dame *Them!* (*Pointing to Vileun*) That's the one! Him with the furry fizzog! He's the one who hip ... hip ... put me in a trance!
Vileun (*moving to Santa, sneering*) *You* are Santa Claus, I presume?
Santa I am he.
Vileun You are my prisoner!

Everyone reacts

Santa Who *are* you?
Vileun I am Vileun the Vile! Master of the Universe! Ha! Ha! Ha!
Dick What do you want with Santa?
Vileun I am taking him back to my planet Varbos!

All react

Listen to me, Earthlings. I have a message for your miserable rulers. Tell them this. If they refuse to accept me as supreme master of the planet Earth, Santa Claus will never return!

All react

The decision is theirs! Vileun the Vile has spoken!
Dame Yes, and what a load of rubbish!
Vileun Silence! *I* am giving the orders!
Dame Then make mine a pint with a pickled onion in it!
Vileun (*to Null and Void*) Take the old fool to the ship!
Dick Santa Claus stays right here!
All (*taking a step towards Vileun threateningly*) Yes!!!
Vileun (*to the audience*) Ha! I'll soon stop their feeble attempts! (*He pulls out his ray gun and points it at the crowd*)

The crowd freeze, except Santa, Roberta, Null and Void

Seize him!

Null and Void move to Santa but Roberta puts up her fists to ward them off
So, my paralysing ray has no effect on·robots! I'll soon deal with that.

Vileun pulls out some of Roberta's wires. She whines and falls on the ground

Santa (*going to her*) Roberta!
Vileun (*to Null and Void*) Take him out!

Null and Void drag Santa out, left

(*To the audience*) Ha! Ha! Told you I'd get him, didn't I? Ha! Ha! Ha!

Vileun exits left, amid boos

The others gradually come back to life

Dame (*dazed*) Cor! What happened? Everything went black. As the house-wife said to the coalman.

Crystal Where's Santa?

Dick They must have taken him to their spaceship! Let's . . . (*he starts to go*)

Tommy Roberta!

They all gather round the fallen robot

2nd Girl They've killed her!

Dick (*kneeling beside Roberta*) I . . . I don't think it's serious. Some of her wires have been pulled out.

Dick replaces the wires and Roberta jumps to her feet, beeping loudly

Roberta Beep! Beep! My master has been kidnapped! Repeat! My master has been kidnapped! Beep!

Dick Quick, everyone! We might still be in time to save Santa!

They all rush to exit, left. A strange, glowing light floods the stage from off left and the sound of the flying saucer taking off is heard. Gradually the light and sounds fade. Everyone turns away from exit, very crestfallen

Crystal (*near to tears*) It's too late . . . They've gone! We'll never see Santa again!

Dick (*comforting her*) Don't upset yourself, Crystal. We'll get him back. There *must* be a way.

Villager How? Vileun's taken him to the planet Varbos. We can't travel through space!

Dame No, I get sea sick taking a bath!

Dick We must get a spaceship!

All A spaceship!!

Dick It's the only way.

Dame I don't wish to be a wet blanket in the ointment but where do we *get* a spaceship? You can't just go into Woollies (*or local shop*) and buy one, you know!

Dick We'll . . . we'll have to *build* one!

Dame Build one! Even if we knew how, it'd take years!

Dick (*defeated*) I know . . . it was a stupid idea!

Roberta (*coming forward and opening the panel in her chest*) Beep! Beep!

Dame Oh, this is no time for gettin' things off your chest, you silly sister to a saucepan, you!

Roberta extracts a toy space rocket and holds it up. Everyone is puzzled

Dick A toy space rocket? What . . .

Roberta goes to the magic cabinet, opens the door and puts the rocket inside. She shuts the door and makes magic passes at the cabinet

That's it! Roberta's right! We'll *magic* a spaceship!

All react

Dame Have you gone dotty, Dicky?
Dick We'll do the same to the toy spaceship as Santa did with the doll. It's worth a try, isn't it?
All Yes!
Dick (*to audience*) Shall I try?

Audience participation

All we have to do is say the magic words and then . . . Oh!
Crystal What's wrong?
Dick I . . . I've forgotten the magic words! (*To others*) Can you remember them?

They all shake their heads

(*To audience*) Can *you* remember the magic words?

Audience participation; hope for the correct response; if not, Roberta or one of the children can say "Hocus Pocus"

That's it! Let's give it a try! You can help as well! (*He goes to the cabinet*) Right! Here goes! After three! One — two — three!
All (*shouting and making magic passes towards the cabinet*) HOCUS POCUS!!!

There is a flash, followed by a Black-out. When the Lights come up a space rocket stands in place of the cabinet

All yell and cheer

Dick It *worked*! (*He opens the rocket door*) All aboard! Next stop, the planet Varbos! We'll rescue Santa and it'll be Christmas this year as usual!
All Hurray!

Song 9 (*All*)

The number ends with Dame Dangle getting stuck in the doorway of the rocket. Dick, Crystal and the children go to her assistance. Roberta gives the impression of drawing main tabs across, waving to the audience as she does so

The CURTAIN *falls*

ACT II

Scene 1

In Outer Space

Full set: the interior of the rocket. This should be as elaborate as possible. At the back is a large, round, observation window. There is a control console with flashing lights, computers, terminals, masses of wiring and tubing, etc., etc. There are entrances right and left

The Villagers and children are discovered, singing and dancing. Roberta at first is busy at the controls then she joins the others in the dance

Song 10 (*Village Children and Roberta*)

Dick and Crystal enter towards the end of the song

Song 11 (*Dick, Crystal and Children*)

After the song Roberta returns to the controls

Villager Captain, how far are we from the planet Varbos?

Dick You'd better ask Roberta. She's the pilot.

Tommy (*going to Roberta*) Can you tell me our position, Roberta?

Roberta Affirmative! We are now entering the planet's stratosphere. Varbos will soon be in sight! Beep!

Children Hurray!

Dick It won't be long now, Crystal. We'll soon have Santa out of Vileun's clutches.

Crystal Oh, Dick, I hope so. When I think of what poor Santa must be going through. He . . . he might even be . . . dead!

Dick No, he's much too valuable a prisoner. Remember, without Santa, Vileun has no hold over the Earth.

2nd Boy Don't you think space travel is fantastic, Captain?

Dick It certainly is!

1st Girl It's like a marvellous dream. Seeing all the planets flying past.

3rd Boy You didn't think it was so marvellous when all those huge meteorites nearly crashed into us! *You* started crying for mummy!

All the boys laugh

Villager Talking of huge meteorites, where's Dame Dangle? We haven't seen her since we took off.

Dick (*laughing*) Ha! Ha! Poor old Aunty's still in her cabin. I don't think the idea of being the first Englishwoman in space appeals to her very much.

2nd Girl (*rushing to Dick*) Captain! I just saw something moving about! Over there! (*She points to entrance left*)

Everyone looks

All (*terrified*) Look! What is it? It's coming this way, (*etc., etc.*)

Dame Dangle lumbers on from the left. She wears an outrageous space costume and helmet. She has the helmet on backwards and can't see where she's going

Tommy *Help!* It's an *alien!!*
Dame (*staggering about*) Oo! Let me out! It's dark in here! Let me out!
Crystal That sounds like . . .
Dick It's Aunty!

Everyone laughs

Dame (*trying to get the helmet off*) Help! Help!
Tommy (*tapping on the helmet*) Hello! Anyone at home?
Dame (*gesturing to the helmet*) Oo! Get me out! It's stuck!

Tommy and Dick tug at helmet

(*Yelling*) Aw! Mind me head! Oh! Be careful! That's me earholes!!

Tommy and Dick pull the helmet off

Oh, that's better! Cor, I could have supplicated in there!

Tommy takes the helmet offstage then returns

Dick What are you dressed up like this for, Aunty?
Dame I found it in me cabin. Rather chick, ain't it? (*She parades about like a mannequin*) It's called the space shuttle look! (*To the audience*) Nice, isn't it? Do you like it? Oh, it really does something for me. Makes me feel like Wonder Woman. *Wonder* Woman, I said dear, not *Blunder* Woman! (*She spins around "Wonder Woman" fashion, then wishes she hadn't*) Oo! Crikey! (*Adjusting her chest*) I think that's unstabled me stabilisers! (*To others*) Aren't you supposed to wear this sort of clobber when you go outer spacing?
Crystal Well, we seem to be managing without.
Dame Ah! But we haven't taken off yet, have we?

All react, unseen by Dame Dangle

You'll all be needing outfits like this when we have lift off. Oh, yes! When we leave Earth's gravy, and go into overdrive and underdrive, not to mention the Whist Drive!
Villager Whist Drive?
Dame I said not to mention that! Then; there's the Galactic Gases! They're pretty 'air raising! Then, you've got to watch out for the hypermarket, that'll crumple yer corsets a bit! Oh, yes! There isn't much you can tell me about space travel! They don't call me the Patrick Moore of (*local town*) for nothin'! You just tell me when we have lift off, and I'll push off!

Dick We've *had* lift off, Aunty. We've been travelling through space for ages.

Dame Oh, that's nice ... (*Double take*) What!?

All (*pointing out front to an imaginary window*) Look!!

Dame (*looking*) Ahh! We're in space! Help! (*She runs up and down in a panic*) Put me down! Let me off! Oo!

Dick Calm down, Aunty.

Dame Calm down! How can I calm down when I'm suspended in space without stays? Oo! I've got no undercarriage! I'm bottomless!

Tommy (*pointing to her rear*) I wouldn't say that!

All the children laugh

Dame Oh, Dick stop this thing! Let me get off! I can't stand heights! I get dizzy on the bathroom scales! Where's the driver? Who's drivin' this heap of scrap iron? I demand to see the driver!

Roberta steps up and salutes

Roberta Beep!

Dame (*in horror*) You! Are *you* the driver?

Roberta Affirmative!

Dame That settles it! Stop the bus!!

Roberta Beep! Impossible! The ship is set on course for Varbos. It cannot be averted! Beep!

Dame (*wailing*) Oo! Beam me down, spotty!!

Crystal You're quite safe, Dame Dangle. You've been in space for some time now and nothing has happened to you, has it?

Dame Oh, I don't know whether I'm on me head or me asteroids! (*Wailing*) I want to go home! Boo hoo! Take me home! (*She cries on Dick's shoulder*)

Villager (*to her*) You want to rescue Santa, don't you?

Dame (*with a sniff*) Yes.

Villager 2 And you want to get even with that nasty Vileun, don't you?

Dame (*sniffing*) Yes! It's just that ... this space travel makes me go all weak at the knees!

Dick Then you need something to take your mind off it. I know! Sing us one of your songs.

Tommy (*gloomily*) Yes, then we can *all* go weak at the knees!

Song 12 (*Dame*)

Roberta (*at controls*) Beep! Attention! Attention! The planet Varbos is now in view!

All rush to look out front. Dame Dangle gets knocked over in the stampede

All Is that it? Varbos! Wow! (*etc., etc.*)

Dame (*pushing in, on hands and knees*) Let's have a butchers! (*Standing up and looking, awestruck*) Cor!

Dick How long before we can land, Roberta?

Roberta Touch down will be in two minutes. Beep!

Tommy Just think in two minutes we'll be setting foot on another world!

Dame Just like goin' to (*local place*)
Villager (*pointing*) Look! What's that?
Villager 2 It's ... it's a fleet of space ships leaving Varbos!
Villager They're heading straight for us!
Dame (*patting her hair*) Oh, how nice! A reception committee.
Roberta Attention! Attention! They are part of Vileun's destructor fleet! We
    are under attack! Repeat! We are under attack!

*There is general panic. Space battle noises are heard, and weird lights flash
across the stage. Everyone is thrown from side to side. All is noise and uproar.
Dame Dangle falls over. Gradually the noises fade and the lights flicker back
to normal*

Dame (*getting up and rubbing her rear*) Oo! I landed right on me Milky
    Way. What happened?
Dick (*dazed*) I ... I don't know. Roberta?
Roberta (*stepping up*) Beep!
Dick What happened to us?
Roberta I have no information. Beep!
Dame Oh, she's about as much use as (*local gag*).
Tommy Listen!

They all stand listening

Dick I can't hear anything.
Tommy That's just it. We've stopped moving!
Roberta Affirmative!
Dick This is Vileun's doing!
Dame Oo! That nasty old no-good! I'd love to get my hands on him!

Vileun enters at the back unseen. He moves behind Dame Dangle

I'd give him a knuckle sandwich right in the breadbasket! Then I'd pull
    out his beard, one hair at a time! Then, I'd—(*To Vileun, absently*) Do
    you know what I'd do then?
Vileun No?
Dame Then I'll tell you ... Eeek! It's *him*!! (*She runs to Dick and hugs him in
    fright*)
Vileun So, miserable Earthlings, we meet again. But not for long. This space
    ship of yours is now under *my* control!
Tommy Oh, no, it isn't!
Vileun Oh, yes it is!
Tommy (*encouraging the audience to join in*) Oh, no it isn't!
Vileun Oh, yes, it is!

This continues for a while

Silence!! (*To the audience*) Shut up, you rabble, or I'll come down there
    and sort you out!

Audience participation

    (*To the others*) This ship of yours is held above the planet Varbos by a powerful beam. Shortly, I will give the command for the beam to be turned off. Then, this rocket, with all of you in it, will be smashed to atoms. Ha! Ha!

Dame Oh! Stop him, Dick! He's goin' to drop us in it!

Vileun You can do nothing! You are powerless! *All* are powerless against Vileun the Vile! Your stupid attempt at rescuing Santa Claus has failed! Farewell, Earthlings! Enjoy your trip *down*! Ha! Ha! Ha!

Vileun exits, laughing

Everyone rushes to Dick

Crystal What are we going to do?

Dick Roberta, is there any way of regaining control of the ship?

Roberta Negative!

Dame (*gulping*) Does ... does that mean we're all going to be smashed to smithereens, like he said?

Dick I'm afraid it looks that way, Aunty.

Dame (*wailing*) Oo! I'm too young to die!!

There is a loud whining noise as the rocket goes into a crash dive. Everyone is yelling and being thrown about. Flashing lights, smoke, etc. There is a loud bang and a flash as the control console blows up. When the noise and commotion is up to full there is a quick Black-out

In the Black-out, a loud explosion is heard as the rocket crashes

SCENE 2

Vileun's Palace on Varbos

Tabs, or the front cloth used in Act I, Scene 1

Vileun enters

Vileun Ha! Ha! Ha! The would-be rescuers from Earth are by now smashed on the rocks of Varbos! Santa Claus is still my prisoner, and will remain so! Oh, I'm clever! Don't you think I'm clever?

Audience participation

Bah! You nothings! Soon I will be your master and you will be my slaves! Ha! Ha! Ha!

Null and Void enter

Nothing can stand in my way now! *Nothing!* (*He turns to exit and bumps into Null and Void*) Ah! Out of my way, you cosmic clodhoppers!

Vileun exits

Void starts singing the carol from Act I, Scene 3

Null Oh, shut up! You sound like (*pop singer*) in the bath!

Void I can't help it, Null. It's that Christmas carol we heard on Earth. I can't get it out of my head.

Null Why not? (*Pointing to Void's head*) There's nothing in there to stop it!

Void I wish there was something we could do to help poor old Santa.

Null Same here. Everytime I pass his cell I have terrible pangs.

Void It's the damp.

Null We're cowards, Void! We ought to stand up to Vileun, and show him our other side.

Void Don't be rude!

Null If only we had the courage of those space heroes. Men like Captain Kirk!

Void Yeah!

Null Buck Rogers!

Void Yeah!

Null Flash Gordon!

Void Yeah—and his brother!

Null Brother?

Void Gay Gordon! Hey! Why don't we ask Superman to help us?

Null No good. He's in *Cape* Town at the moment. We could ask Batman, I suppose.

Void No, the Batmobile's having its MOT. There's always Spider Man.

Null No, he's a crawler! What about Wonder Woman?

Void (*leering*) Yeah! What *about* Wonder Woman? Cor!!

Null How about asking the Incredible Hulk?

Void No, I don't think Cyril Smith would help us.

Astra enters in mystic fashion, hands on forehead and moaning deeply

Astra Ooooh!

Null Look out! Here comes Nightmare Nellie!

Astra (*moving between them*) I have just had a meditation!

Null (*jumping away*) Ugh! Is it catching?

Astra I have been in contact with long dead beings.

Void What, the (*local football team or council*)?

Astra (*waving her arms upwards and moaning in comedy/mystic fashion*) Ooo! Ooo! The stars! The stars! I have consulted the stars!

Null Get any autographs?

Astra (*on another planet*) The stars! They tell me everything! They are my guides to the mysteries of the Universe. The stars! (*She starts swaying*) Ooo! I feel a manifestation coming on!

Void It's probably wind.

Astra The stars told me I would meet someone! Someone who will show me the way. Ooo! The vibrations! I feel the vibrations!

Astra sways from side to side. Null and Void do the same

He is *here*! The one the stars told me of! He is *here*! Ooo! (*She starts turning on the spot*)

Null (*to the audience*) It's all right. She's just having a turn!

Astra (*suddenly stopping, turning and pointing dramatically at Void*) You! It is *you*!

Void Eeek! I'm off! (*He starts to exit*)
Astra (*in a voice of doom*) Stop!

Void stops dead in his tracks

Stand still! (*She drifts towards him*) Let me feel your aura.
Void (*backing away*) Ger' off!
Astra Be still! I command it!

Astra grabs Void and holds him very close. He looks towards the audience, a picture of absolute terror

Void (*in a high-pitched squeal*) Mummy!!
Astra (*holding Void away from her but not letting him go*) Yes! It *is* you! *You* are the one!
Null Oh, he's a right one all right!
Astra (*to Void*) Come to me!

Astra swings Void around so that his back is to the audience and she is above him. She slowly runs her hands down his back. When she gets to his bottom Void reaches around and pushes her hands back up

Astra Ah, yes! I can feel the power surging through you! (*Holding Void away from her*) You shall be my conductor!
Void Any more fares, please?
Astra The stars told me of your coming. A *star* never lies!
Null No, but there's a better Page Three in the *Sun*. Boom! Boom!
Astra (*swinging Void to face front*) Show me!
Void Eh?
Astra Show me the way!
Void Oh! (*Pointing to auditorium*) Well, you go down here and—(*he gives directions to the ladies'*)
Astra (*holding out her hand*) Take my hand!
Void (*taking it and singing*) "I'm a stranger in paradise" . . .
Astra Let our powers mingle! (*She grabs both Void's hands and starts moaning*) Ooo! Ooo!
Void (*deadpan*) Mingle . . . mingle . . . mingle.
Astra (*pushing Void away*) Ah! I am about to have a vision! (*She puts her hands to her forehead and closes her eyes*) Something is emerging from the dark beyond! (*She goes into a trance*)

Comic business as Void turns away to inspect his clothes

(*In a trance*) Ooo! A picture is forming! I see it! Oo! . . . Ah! . . . Oh! . . . Mmm! . . . Ahh!
Null ⎫ (*together*) ⎱ Bisto!
Void ⎭   ⎰
Astra Oo! The picture starts to fade!
Null Call— (*local TV shop*).
Astra It is gone! Gone!

Astra's head and arms drop. She remains motionless and silent. Null and Void look at her, then at the audience, then back to Astra. They shrug and start sauntering up and down, whistling, looking at watches, etc.

Null (*at last, to the audience*) Don't go to sleep will you?

Null and Void look at Astra

Void This is worse than the intervals on Channel Four!
Astra (*suddenly looking up*) Ahh!

Null and Void jump

Astra Oh, *what* a vision! *What* a vision! Strange, I am never at my best when the moon is on the wane.
Null You're never at your best whether it's *waning* or shining!
Astra I must find my master at once. The mighty Vileun will derive great pleasure from what I have just seen.

Vileun enters

Master! O, Diabolical One! I have just had a vision!
Vileun Well?
Astra I saw the space rocket from Earth!
Vileun Yes, yes?
Astra I saw it fall from the skies and shatter into dust on the planet's surface!
Vileun Ha! Ha! Ha! Splendid! So perish all who would oppose Vileun the Vile! (*To Astra*) Go and investigate the wreckage. And if you find any survivors—you know what to do!

Vileun and Astra make throat slitting gestures

Astra exits, cackling

Vileun (*to Null and Void*) Bring Santa Claus to me! And not a word of what has happened! Go!

Null and Void run out

(*To the audience*) Ha! Ha! Ha! I can't wait to see the old fool's face when I tell him I have destroyed his would-be rescuers! Ha! Ha! Ha!

Null and Void enter with Santa between them

Ah! My dear Santa Claus! How are you enjoying your stay? Is your cell comfortable? Do you like the rats? We have enormous rats on Varbos, don't you agree?
Santa Yes, and I'm looking at the biggest one now!

Null and Void roar with laughter

Vileun Silence, scum! (*To the audience*) And you! (*To Santa*) I have something to tell you, Santa.
Santa Yes, and I have something to tell *you*. Return me to Earth at once!
Vileun Ha! Ha! My dear fat friend, you will only return to Earth if they accept me as their Lord and Master!

Santa Earth will never surrender to you!

Vileun Then it looks as if you'll be ending your days here on Varbos. (*Sneering*) But perhaps you have hopes of being rescued, eh?

Santa I want no-one hurt on my account.

Vileun Ha! A little late for such sentiment. I have already destroyed one rescue party!

Santa Oh, no!

Vileun Oh, yes! They are little more than dust by now! Ha! Ha! Ha!

Astra rushes in, in great alarm

Astra Master! Master! O, Infamous One! The Earthlings managed to escape the crash and have disappeared!

Vileun (*enraged*) *What!?*

Santa

Null } (*together*) { Hurray!!

Void

Vileun Great blistering blobs of bilge! They must be captured at once!

Astra There is no need, your Spitefulness! Tracks show that they have entered the Wilderlands! Nothing can survive there!

Vileun (*gloating*) You are right!

Astra I managed to capture one of the Earthlings.

Vileun Splendid! Bring it to Me!

Astra exits

(*to Santa*) So, it seems your foolhardy friends have escaped death, but not for long! The Wilderlands of Varbos are treacherous! They will *soon* be dead, if they are not already!

Astra enters, dragging in a very bedraggled Dame Dangle

Dame Take your hands off me, you punk rocker, you!

Santa Dame Dangle!

Dame (*turning and seeing him*) Santa! It's dear old Santa!

Overjoyed, Dame Dangle rushes towards Santa. Vileun steps in front of her

Oh, no! It's JR (*or popular TV villain*) again!

Vileun You are my prisoner!

Dame Oh! . . . Go and disappear up your own black hole!

Santa How did you manage to escape the crash?

Dame Oh, it was terrible! Terrible! (*To the audience*) It really was! I never want to go through that again, not if I live to be . . . er . . . twenty-five! I'm black and blue all over! I've got bruises as big as dinner plates! I bet you'd like to see 'em, wouldn't you? Well, you're not goin' to! You're much too young for X films! How we weren't all deaded, beats me. I was a terrible wreck. We all climbed out, and went explorin'. I got lost, silly me! The next thing I know, old Toyah Wilcox (*or punk rock singer*) over there grabs me, and here I am! (*To Vileun*) You just wait till my nephew get his hands on you! You'll be Vileun the *Pile*, then!

Vileun Ha! Your nephew and the other fools are doomed. They have entered a place from which there is no return.

Dame Oh, no! They haven't gone into the (*local night spot or public hall*)?

Vileun They will all die in the dreaded Wilderlands!

Dame (*wailing*) Oooo!

Santa Don't worry, Dame Dangle. Something will turn up.

Vileun Ha! The only thing that's going to turn up is her toes! (*He takes hold of Santa*) Come, Santa, back to your nice cell! (*To Null and Void*) Guard her well until I have devised a suitably painful death for her! Ha! Ha! Ha!

Dame Ooo!

Vileun and Astra drag Santa out, laughing their terrible laughs

Dame Dangle is blubbering and wailing. She searchs for her hanky under her knicker leg. Null and Void find this very funny

Null (*to the audience, pointing to Dame Dangle's bloomers*) Look! It's rent-a-tent!

Dame Dangle continues to search for a hanky. Void takes out his own hanky and hands it to Dame. She blows into it very loudly then hands it back to Void. He opens it. There is an enormous round hole in the middle. Null roars with laughter

Void (*pocketing the hanky*) Don't laugh! Can't you see she's upset? (*He puts his arm around Dame*) There, there. Don't cry!

Dame Dangle pushes Void away and he falls over

Dame (*wailing*) Booo hooo!!

Null I wish there was something we could do to cheer her up.

Void I know! Let's have a sing song!

Null Good thinking, Batman! (*To audience*) You'll join us in a sing song, won't you? All the girls and boys —

Void And mums and dads!

Null And the grans and grandads!

Void And the aunties and nunkies!

Null (*pointing to a section of audience*) And you lot, down there, hiding! Don't think you're going to get away with it! Now, are you all going to sing? (*Audience participation*) I can't hear you! I said, are you going to sing? (*When audience shout back*) That's better! (*To Dame Dangle*) Isn't that nice, Dame Dangle? Everyone out there's going to sing to you. Doesn't that make you feel better?

Dame (*with a sniff*) A bit! What are they going to sing?

Null Well, it just so happens—surprise! surprise!—we've got some words here!

The song sheet can be handed in from the wings or can descend from above. It should be an "Old MacDonald" style song. If song sheet is handed on Void can hold it upside down, etc.

Dame (*to audience*) Can you see it at the back? No? Well, what are you doing and stop it at once! Right, here goes! (*To conductor or pianist*) Ready when you are, Andre Privet!

Song 13 (*Audience Participation Song—Dame, Null and Void*)

Half way through the number Dame Dangle stops everyone

Hang on! Hold it! Wow! (*To Null*) I thought you said they were *all* going to sing! I can't hear the kiddie-winkies!

Null } (*together*) { The kiddie winkies!
Void }

Dame They're not singing! (*To the audience*) You kiddie-winkies, you're not singing, are you?

Audience participation "Oh, no you're not!" "Oh, yes, we are!" etc

I don't believe you! (*To Null and Void*) They're a lot of little fibbers!

Null There's only one way to find out! Let's get some of 'em up here!

Null and Void go down into audience, collect some children and take them on stage

Dame (*to children, ad lib*) What's your name? (*etc., etc.*) Now then, my little Pavagrotties! Let's see if you can sing or not! Music, maestro, please!

The number continues and ends

(*To the audience*) Let's give them a great big hand!

A four foot cut-out of a hand appears from the wings. Void takes it and staggers over to present it to the children, comic business. Dame Dangle chases him off with the hand. They return immediately with sweets, which they hand out to the children. Null starts the applause then he and Void take the children back to their seats. Dame Dangle waves goodbye then starts crying again. Null and Void return to stage

Null Oh, look! She's turned the taps on again!

Dame Ooo! I shall never see my friends again! Boo hoo!

Null (*taking Void to one side*) Now's our chance! Let's help her find her friends. With their help we might be able to defeat Vileun. Let's desert!

Void What, before we've had the main meal?

Null (*going to Dame*) Listen. We hate old Vileun. We'll take you to the Wilderlands and help you find your friends. Won't we, Void?

Void (*shaking*) I . . . I'm not going to the Wilderlands! There's a m . . . m . . . monster there!

Dame (*overjoyed*) Oh, you'll help me! Oh, you adorable aliens, you! (*She hugs and kisses them*)

Null (*to Void, pulling a face*) And you're worried about a monster!

Dame (*coming forward, dramatically*) Come! What are we waiting for! Let us take this giant step for mankind! Forward! To the Wilderlands!

Dame Dangle marchs to the exit. Null whistles. Dame stops and turns. Null indicates the exit on the opposite side

Oh, what a silly billy I am!

Dame Dangle exits as indicated. Null follows her. Void creeps to other side

Null grabs him and hauls him out, as the Lights fade to a Black-out

SCENE 3

The Wilderlands of Varbos

Full set. A strange, bluish landscape. Tall, odd-shaped rocks tower on each side. At the back is a ground row of low rocks and weird-looking plants. The back cloth shows the planet's surface under a multi-coloured sky with a ridge of jagged mountains in the far distance

To open, suitable music with special lighting and perhaps ground mist. The Varborites creep on from different directions, one or two at a time. They meet in the middle and go into their strange dance

Song 14 (*Varborites' dance*)

After the dance, the Varborites stand in groups, talking. The Leader calls them to order

Leader Varborites! We must not linger in this dreadful place. Remember these are the Wilderlands—the home of the monster! We must leave here at once, unless you want to be its dinner!

2nd Varborite How do *you* know it eats people?

3rd Varborite Yes, *I've* never seen it eating *people*!

Leader Tell me, have you ever been near enough to see *what* it's eating?

Varborites True!

The Monster's roar is heard on the offstage microphone

(*All cowering downstage*) *The monster!!!*

The Monster of the Wilderness lumbers into view at the back

It sees the terrified group of Varborites and lumbers down to them, emitting a deep growl. They turn, slowly, and are paralysed with fear at the sight of the Monster. It holds out its paw to one group of Varborites and makes growling noises. It is obviously trying to communicate. The group of Varborites yell, and run out. The Monster turns to the other group and repeats its actions. That group yells and runs out. The Monster, left alone, shrugs its shaggy shoulders and gives a great pitiful sigh. This may get reactions from Audience, such as "Aaaaah! Poor thing, etc." It sees the Audience and comes forward, holding out its paws and growling, trying to communicate. This fails and it turns away, going into a sad-comic dance

Song 15 (*Monster dance*)

The Monster lumbers off at the back, very down hearted

Dick (*off, calling*) Aunty! Where are you?

Crystal (*off, calling*) Dame Dangle! Where are you?

Dick, Crystal, Roberta, Tommy, the Villagers and Children enter from the same side. All are footsore and weary

Dick (*looking about, and calling*) Aunty!
All (*calling*) Dame Dangle! Where are you?
Dick (*with a sigh*) Nothing! (*To the others*) Let's rest a while.

They all flop to the ground, exhausted. Roberta takes out a small oil can and drinks from it. Dick and Crystal come forward

Crystal Oh, Dick, we've walked miles and miles with no sign of Dame Dangle. What could have happened to her?
Dick I wish I knew, Crystal. Oh, if only I'd kept a closer watch on her after we left the wreck! As a solider I should have been better organized. Now we've got *two* problems! Rescuing Santa and finding Aunty!
Tommy (*coming down to Dick*) Captain! I . . . I don't like this place! There's something spooky about it! I . . . I'm sure I saw something moving about, over there! (*He points to the rocks at the back*)

The 1st Girl screams and starts wailing. Crystal goes to comfort her

Dick Now then, Tommy! Don't go frightening everyone. It's bad enough being stranded on a strange planet without you giving us the willies! (*To the others*) Come on! This won't find Dame Dangle! Up you get!

They all get to their feet, wearily. The Monster's roar is heard on the offstage microphone. Everyone huddles in a terrified group

Crystal (*clinging to Dick*) What was *that*?
Dick I don't know but it didn't sound very friendly.

The Varborites creep on at the back, unseen by the others

Tommy I . . . told you this place was spooky!
Villager Captain, let's get away from here!
Dick I think that's a good idea.

They start to exit

Villager (*seeing Varborites*) Look!

They all look. The Varborites, in a huddle, cower away

Crystal (*to Dick*) Who *are* they?
Dick I'll find out. (*He moves to the Varborites, who shrink back*) It's all right. I'm not going to hurt you. We're from the planet Earth.

Dick moves to the Varborites again, but again they shrink back

Crystal The poor things seem terrified. Let me try.

Crystal moves to the Varborites and sings

Song 16 (*Crystal*)

During the song Crystal wins the Varborites over. She encourages them to shake hands with Dick and the others. By the end they are all singing together, the best of friends

1st Varborite People of Earth, we welcome you to Varbos. Forgive our apprehension, but we have grown to be wary of strangers. (*Sadly*) Our planet is not what it used to be. A black cloud of evilness has descended on our world.

Dick In the shape of Vileun the Vile!

5th Varborite You know of him?

Dick Yes. He is the reason for our being here.

Tommy He kidnapped Santa Claus!

Varborites (*puzzled*) Santa Claus?

Crystal He is a dear friend to everyone on our planet.

Dick And it's imperative that he returns to Earth before next week. Can you help us rescue him!

1st Varborite (*sighing*) I fear not. Vileun is much too powerful. Only one man has the knowledge to destroy him.

Dick Who?

Leader Prince Paragon!

The Varborites salute

Dick Then take us to him.

1st Varborite If only we could. Prince Paragon ruled this planet, as his father did before him, with great kindness and justice. When Vileun came, our Prince discovered the secret of his destruction, but before he could set about it, Vileun made him vanish into thin air. He has not been seen from that sad day to this. We Varborites were forced to run and hide.

Dick A sad tale indeed. But at least we now know that there *is* a way of destroying Vileun. Somehow we must find that way.

1st Varborite Do you mean you are willing to help rid Varbos of his evil presence?

Villagers, etc Aye!

The Varborites express their thanks

Dick But first, we need your help in finding one of our company who is missing.

6th Varborite We have seen no other strangers but you.

4th Varborite We had best find your friend soon, before ... before ...

Dick Yes?

2nd Varborite Before something *else* does!

The Monster's roar is heard on the offstage microphone

Crystal That noise again! What is it?

1st Varborite It is the cry of the Monster of the Wilderlands! I suggest we look for your friend this way.

Dick Very well! Lead on!

The Varborites exit, followed by the others

After a slight pause Dame Dangle creeps on backwards from left and Void creeps on backwards from right. In the centre their posteriors touch

Dame Oo! I think I'm having a close encounter!

Comic business as Dame and Void turn to face each other

Null enters

Null No sign of 'em that way.

Dame Oh! All this walking! I've got bunions as big as globe artichokes and me athlete's foot is playing up something chronic!

Void Give it back to him then.

Dame (*hobbling down*) I'm going to have a sit down! (*She sits on the ground*)

Null You can't stop *here*! These are the Wilderlands!

Dame I don't care if it's double yellow lines! I'm havin' a rest! (*To audience*) Oh! It's good to take the weight off me whatnot! Now to inspect me poor old tootsies! (*She pulls off her boot and rubs her foot*) Oh, look at that foot! It feels like a deep fried doughnut!

Void (*very scared*) Let's ... let's get away from here!

Dame Oh, shut up do! I've got to get me red corporals flowin' again! (*She holds up her boot and a large rock falls out*) Cor! Look at that! No wonder I've been havin' trouble. I'll keep this as a chiffonier of our trip! (*She puts the rock in her bag and replaces her boot*) Now for a bit of shut eye! (*She lies full length on the ground*)

Void (*standing over her*) Dame Dangle, come on!

Dame Cooo! I can see right up your nose! Talk about black holes!

Null This place is dangerous!

Void There's something here that's huge, horrible and hairy!

Dame I know. But I've got used to your nose now.

Null There's a ... *monster*!

Dame (*sitting up*) A monster? Ha! Fiddlesticks! There's no such thing as monsters! (*To audience*) Is there?

Audience participation—"Oh, yes there is"; "oh, no there isn't"; etc

Well, *I* don't believe in 'em! You two go and look for the others! I'll catch you up when I've had me little rest!

Void You'll get lost!

Dame Lost? Me? Rubbish! I've got a wonderful sense of dissection. I've got a built in compress! Now, *push off* and let me have a kip! (*She lies down*)

Null and Void shrug their shoulders at the audience, then exit

(*Getting comfy on the ground*) Monsters indeed! What nonsense! (*To the audience*) Just in case ... if you *do* see anything ... give us a shout, won't you? Ta, very much! Night, night! (*She curls up and falls asleep with her thumb in her mouth. She snores loudly*)

The Monster appears at the back

It sees the Dame and lumbers down to her. The audience will be shouting "Wake up! It's the monster", etc., etc. Dame wakes up, not seeing the Monster

(*To audience*) What is it! (*Getting to her feet*) What? A *monster*! Where? ("*Behind you!*" etc.) Behind me!

Comic business with Dame Dangle turning around and the Monster turning at the same time. Dame Dangle faces the audience again

You're havin' me on! There's nothing there! Oh, you rotten lot! Waking me up for nothing, I . . .

The Monster puts its paw on Dame Dangle's shoulder. Agog, she reaches up and strokes the paw

I . . . I think I'm havin' a close encounter of the *furred* kind! (*She slowly turns and comes face to face with the monster*) Aaaaah!!

Dame Dangle jumps in the air and runs to one side. The Monster lumbers towards her

Help! Save me! Oo! Keep away from me, you hairy horror! Help! Help! (*She slides to the ground*)

Dick, Crystal, Roberta, Tommy, the Villagers and Children and Varborites, rush on

Dick Aunty! (*He rushes over and hauls the Monster away from Dame Dangle*)
Crystal Dick! Be careful!

The Monster offers no resistance. It turns to Dick with its paws held out

Monster (*trying to communicate*) Gerrah! Urrrah!
Crystal I . . . I think it's trying to talk.

The Monster nods its head eagerly. Everyone reacts

Monster Gerrah! Gerrah!
Tommy What's it trying to say?
Dame I can't understand a flippin' word! It must come from (*neighbouring town or village*)
Dick (*to the Monster, slowly*) Do—you—understand—me?

The Monster nods vigorously

Crystal What—is—your—name?
Monster Errrah!
Dame *Ernie!* It doesn't look like an Ernie to me! Looks more like a Harry! (*She pronounces it "Hairy"*)
Dick Roberta, perhaps *you* can interpret for us.
Roberta Beep! I will try! (*She moves to the Monster*) Beeeep! Bip! Deee Beeeep! Dip bip?

The Monster shakes its head. Roberta turns to Dick and shrugs her shoulders

Negative!
Crystal I've got an idea. Santa taught me some magic words to use on the Reindeer when we wanted them to communicate with us. I'll see if that works. (*She goes to the Monster*) O, creature, be you fierce or meek—I bestow on you the power to speak!

On the last word Roberta makes magic passes at the Monster. It staggers, clutching at its throat and coughing

Dame Now you've given it whoopin' cough!
Monster (*after a loud clearing of its throat*) H ... Hello!
Crystal It worked!

There is general delight

 Null and Void enter at the back and stand listening unseen by the others

Monster (*overjoyed*) I can *speak*! Ha! Ha! I can *talk* again! I can *speak*! (*He shakes Crystal warmly by the hand*) A thousands thanks to you! (*He shakes Dick's hand*) And to you! (*He makes for Dame Dangle*) And to you! (*He offers his paw*)
Dame (*pulling her hand away*) Not until you've cut them toe nails!
Dick (*to the Monster*) Now you can tell us who you are.
Monster Certainly! (*With great dignity*) I am Prince Paragon of Varbos!

All react. The Varborites drop to their knees

1st Varborite Your Highness! We ... we thought you were dead!
Monster I might as well have been. Oh, a monster's life is a miserable one indeed! Rise!

The Varborites get to their feet

I have tried to approach you many times but you always fled from me. Not that I blame you. My appearance is unattractive to say the least.
3rd Varborite Did Vileun do *this* (*indicating the Monster's shape*) to you, your Highness?
Monster He did! At the very moment I was about to destroy him, he changed me into what you see! A hideous, lumbering monster, devoid of speech! But now, thanks to these good strangers, my voice shall be heard again! (*Sadly*) But alas, a *voice* is not enough. A man of action is needed and being this awkward shape, I am somewhat hampered.
Dick Prince Paragon, tell *us* how to destroy Vileun, and it's as good as done!
Villagers Aye!
Monster Earth people, you are very courageous, but ridding our planet of Vileun is *my* responsibility.
Dick He is holding our friend Santa Clause captive. *His* rescue is *our* responsibility. If we destroy Vileun at the same time, so much the better!
Villagers Aye!
Monster So be it! And if you succeed, I shall be for ever in your debt. Listen then and I will tell you how to bring about Vileun's destruction.

Everyone gathers around the Monster

 All his power lies in an amulet, a magical stone that he keeps on a chain around his neck. Remove the stone and Vileun will vanish like stars in daylight!
Dame But how are we going to do that? You can't get near the old frump face!

Tommy Couldn't we take the stone while he's asleep?
Monster Vileun the Vile never sleeps!
Dame Oh, the dirty old stop out!

Null and Void move down to the others

Null Excuse us!
Roberta Beep! Beep! We are under attack! Beep! (*She charges at Null and Void with her fists up*)
Dame (*pulling Roberta back*) It's all right! Keep your tin lid on! They're on our side now! They helped me escape!
Null (*to Dick*) Void and I want to offer our services. If we can help you get rid of old face-ache, we will!
Void Yes! Just tell us what to do!
Dame We have to get into Vileun's palace and remove his gall stone!
Dick I have a plan! (*To Null and Void*) And with *your* help, it should work! Gather round, everyone!

They all gather around Dick as the Lights fade to a Black-out

SCENE 4

Vileun's Palace

Tabs, or front cloth used in Act II, Scene 2

Vileun enters. He lifts his amulet and gazes at it adoringly

Vileun O, amulet of abominable authority! O, stone of sinister secret! Together we shall rule the entire Universe! Oh, yes we will!

Audience participation

(*To the stone*) No one knows your secret. Only the fool Prince Paragon guessed your true power and I changed him into a speechless monster! Ha! Ha! Ha! Your secret is safe! No one shall take you from me! Ha! Ha! Ha!

Astra enters and coughs

Vileun, in mid cackle, chokes

Astra O, your Callousness, I beg forgiveness for disturbing your cackle but I have news.
Vileun What is it?
Astra Null and Void are here.
Vileun (*enraged*) What! Those traitors! Those deserters! I'll have them ... (*He starts to go*)
Astra (*stopping him*) No, your Hatefulness. It seems we misjudged them. It appears they only pretended to desert in order to gain the confidence of the Earthlings.
Vileun Why?
Astra So that they could capture them!

Vileun Ha! Ha! The cunning clots! Have they been successful?

Astra Indeed, your Vileness! (*Gloating*) They have taken four Earthlings prisoner!

Vileun Splendid! Splendid! Have them brought in!

Astra (*calling off*) Bring in the prisoners!

Vileun and Astra move to one side

Null (*off*) Prisoners, quick march! Hup! Hup! Hup!

Dick, Tommy and Roberta march in, followed by Null

Hup! Hup! Prisoners—Halt!

They halt in a line. Null gives Vileun a salute and marches to the back

Dame Dangle enters, being frog-marched by Void

Dame (*pushing Void away*) Remove your paws from my posterior!

Void pushes her over to the others, then gives Vileun a comic salute and joins Null at the back. Vileun moves over to inspect the line of prisoners

Vileun Well, well, well! The would-be rescuers from Earth, my prisoners once more! (*To Dame Dangle*) What have you to say for yourself?

Dame I shall only give my name, rank and telephone number!

Vileun I see. (*He moves away*) So, you have nothing to say, before I . . . (*he turns quickly, pulling out a ray gun*) . . . execute you! (*He levels the gun at them*)

Dame Oo! He's goin' to split our atoms!

Dick (*stepping forward*) Vileun, hear me. I've been doing a lot of thinking since we landed on Varbos. At first I thought you were just a villain but now I realize that you are a very clever man. A genius! A mastermind!

Dame Yes! A right little Magnus Mackeson!

Vileun (*to Dick*) Go on. I like what I am hearing.

Dick Your plan to rule the Universe—A masterpiece! A tremendous feat!

Dame (*pointing to Vileun's feet*) Yes, I've never seen such whopping great wellie warmers!

Dick It would be an honour to serve under such a man as you.

Vileun (*flattered, but puzzled*) Am I to understand that you wish to join me?

Dick (*with a bow*) If your Majesty will have me. (*He returns to the line*)

Vileun Mm! And what of your companions? Are they of the same mind? (*He goes to Roberta*) What about you, Metal Mickey?

Roberta Beep! It would be an honour to serve under you.

Vileun (*to Tommy*) And you?

Tommy It would be an honour to serve under you. (*He gives a salute*)

Vileun (*to Dame*) And *you*?

Dame (*gushing*) Oh! It would be an honour to serve under, over and round the back of you! Oh! I want to be your right-hand man! I'll be Tonto to your Lone Ranger! Robin to your Batman! Denis to your Maggie! Tony to your Benn—and Marks to your Spencer!

Dick (*to Vileun*) You see, we all wish to bask in your greatness.

Dame Yes and I'm the biggest basket of 'em all!

Vileun But what of your friend Santa Claus? You came to Varbos to rescue him, did you not?

Dick Ha! We have no use for him!

Tommy He's a silly old fool!

Roberta Hear! Hear!

Dame I hope his beard chokes him!

Vileun and Astra enjoy this

Vilelun Ha! Ha! Ha! I like it! Oh, he must hear this for himself! He is under the impression that all Earthlings love him! Ha! Ha! (*To Astra*) Bring Santa Claus here.

Astra exits, gloating

Dame (*sidling up to Vileun, seductively*) Oh, how wonderful it must be to have a brain like yours. I wish I had one.

Vileun Yes, one needs a superior brain if one is to conquer a Universe.

Dame (*"posh" voice*) Oh, yus! One does, doesn't one! I used to be a dab 'and at conquerin' meself, you know! When hi was hat school—a couple of years ago—hi was the best hin my class! Oh, hi was conquerin' hall the time! (*She mimes playing conkers*) I've still got a smashin' pair of sixers— (*She snuggles up to Vileun, fluttering her eyelashes*)—If you'd like to see 'em. (*She sees the amulet around his neck*) Oo! What a stiffin' starkler! May I 'ave a butchers?

Dame makes a grab for the amulet but Vileun pushes her back to the others

Vileun Get your hands off my amulet!

Astra enters with Santa, who does not see the others

Vileun Ah, Santa! I have a surprise for you. Some of your *friends* are here! (*He points to the line*)

Santa (*overjoyed, rushing to them*) My dear friends!

The four put their noses in the air

(*Puzzled*) Er . . . Roberta!

Roberta blows a loud raspberry at Santa

Tommy!

Tommy sticks his tongue out

Dame Dangle!

Dame Push off, you old poop-face!

Santa (*very disturbed by now*) Captain Daring?

Dick Don't bother me, you old goat!

Santa (*moving nearer to them*) My friends!

The four turn their backs on Santa

But . . . what have I done! . . . tell me . . . what have I done!

Vileun (*gloating*) Well, Santa, it seems you are not as popular as you thought. Your so called friends have seen sense and have decided to join *me*!

Santa (*horrified*) What? I ... I don't believe it! (*To the others, who still have their backs to him*) Roberta? ... Captain? ... This isn't true, is it? You haven't joined this dastardly devil, have you?

Dame
Dick } (*together turning*) Yes!
Roberta
Tommy

Santa (*shattered*) Oh, dear, oh dear, oh dear!

Dick (*pushing Santa aside and going to Vileun*) Master, now that we have joined your legions, wouldn't a toast be in order?

Vileun A capital idea! A toast to our partnership! I have an excellent vintage vino from Venus!

Dame Make mine a pint of plonk from Pluto!

Vileun (*to Null, indicating Santa*) Take the old fool back to his cell!

Null (*rubbing his hands in devilish fashion*) Wouldn't it be *nastier* to let him stay and watch the toast? Think how humiliating it will be! (*He cackles*) He! He! He!

Vileun, then Astra start cackling. Dame Dangle joins in, followed by Dick, Roberta and Tommy. Void, not to be outdone, starts up with his idea of a cackle, a high pitched, whinnying noise. On hearing this, the others stop and look at him. Void becomes aware of this, and his "laughter" drifts slowly into a nervous cough

Vileun (*to Null*) Yes, you are right! Let him remain!

Vileun and Astra exit

As soon as they are out of sight, everyone rushes to Santa. Roberta hugs him

Santa (*dismayed*) But ...

Dick Sorry for being rude to you just now, Santa, but it was part of our plan.

Santa Plan?

Tommy Yes, to destroy Vileun.

Dame We're all in on it. Even Hinge and Bracket (*or a popular duo*) over there! (*She points to Null and Void*)

Santa But, how are you going to do it?

Dick The source of Vileun's power lies in that stone he wears around his neck. Once we get *that*, he's finished! (*Taking out a small bottle*) The Varborites gave us this drug! We're going to put it in his drink. That's why I suggested the toast.

Santa How are you going to do that without him seeing you?

Dick (*stumped*) I ... I hadn't thought of that.

Dame I know! We'll have to create a nasturtium!

All A what!

Null I think she means a *diversion*!

Dame That's what I said, you extra-terrestial twit!

Dick You're right, Aunty! A diversion! Something to attract Vileun's attention. But what!

Dame A loud noise! That's what we need! (*To Void*) Can you make a loud noise?

Void (*shyly, indicating the audience*) Not in front of all these people.

Dame (*pointing to the audience*) We'll get *them* to help us! (*To the audience*) You'll help us, won't you?

Audience participation

Good! Now, here's what I want you to do. When I say—"Cheers", you all shout—"Bottom's up!" Do you think you can do that? Well, let's have a practice. Here goes! Cheers!

The audience shout back

(*To the others*) Did you hear anything? No, that wasn't very good! Try again, and take the roof off! CHEERS!

The audience shout back

That's more like it! Now, remember, when I say cheers you all shout ...

The audience shout

Spot on! (*To Dick*) While old nasty's looking to see where the noise is coming from, you drig his drunk ... I mean, drug his drink!

Dick Right!

Roberta (*looking off*) Beep! Beep! They are returning!

They all rush back to their former positions and pretend to jeer Santa

Vileun and Astra enter. She carries a tray with two weird-looking goblets on it

Vileun Now for the toast! (*He takes the two goblets and hands one to Dick*) Let us drink to the domination of the Universe! (*He holds up his goblet to Dick*)

Dick (*holding up his goblet*) To the domination of the Universe!

Dame (*loudly, giving the audience their cue*) CHEERS!

The audience shout "Bottoms up". Vileun does not take any notice

Coo! (*To Vileun*) Did you hear that?

Vileun (*unmoved*) What?

Dame It ... it sounded like a lot of people shoutin' "Bottoms up!"

Vileun I heard nothing! On with the toast! (*He holds up his goblet to Dick*) To the domination of the Universe!

Dick (*holding up his goblet*) To the domination of the Universe!

Dame (*very loudly; encouraging the audience to be loud*) CHEERS!

The audience shout "Bottoms up". This time Vileun hears it, but continues to look at Dick

Vileun What on *Mars* was that?

Dame It seemed to come from out there! (*She points to the audience*)
Vileun (*looking anywhere but at the audience*) Out *where*?
All (*pointing to the audience*) Out there!
Vileun (*looking out front*) Out *there*?

Vileun and Astra peer out at the audience. Dick quickly pours the drug into Vileun's drink

I can see nothing! (*Turning and holding up his goblet*) The toast! To the domination of the Universe!
Dick (*holding up his goblet*) To the domination of the Universe!

Vileun and Dick drink. All are watching Vileun. He takes Dick's goblet and puts it, with his own, on the tray

Astra exits to remove tray and returns immediately

Dame Dangle, who has been leaning forward watching Vileun, almost falls over

Vileun Our partnership is sealed! We ... (*puzzled*) What are you all staring at? Ah, dazzled by my magnificence, eh? Well, I don't blame you! I ... (*He puts his hand to his head and staggers about*) I ... feel ... dizzy ...
Tommy (*to the others*) It's working!
Astra (*rushing to Vileun*) Master!

Null and Void grab Astra and hold her away from Vileun

Vileun (*making a weak grab for Dick*) You ... tricked me! ... Ahhh! (*His arms fall to his sides, and his head drops forward. He stands still and silent*)
Dame Now, Dick! Get the stone!

Dick moves to Vileun and cautiously reaches for the amulet. He is just about to touch it when Vileun's hand shoots up and grabs the stone. He gives a great bellow of triumphant laughter. Dick and the others fall back. Null and Void release Astra and run to the others. Vileun and Astra are one side of the stage, the frightened group on the other

Astra You *fools*! With my telepathic powers I read your minds and told my master of your puny little plan!
Vileun Ha! Ha! Ha! Your pathetic drug had no effect on me! *I* am immune to such puny potions! But you have somehow discovered the secret of my amulet and for that—you must all die!

The others cling to each other in terror

Astra (*with great relish*) Let me destroy them with a shower of flaming meteors!
Vileun No! *I* shall kill them myself! One at a time! (*He pulls out his ray gun*) Starting with—(*To the audience*) Which one shall I kill first?

Audience participation

I think I'll start with ... the *fat* one! (*He points to Dame Dangle*)

The others jump away from Dame Dangle leaving her on her own, shaking with fear

Dame (*wailing*) Ooo! Why does it always have to be *me*!! (*She covers her eyes*)

Vileun (*aiming his gun*) Prepare to die, Earth woman!

Suddenly Roberta steps out of the group and goes to Vileun

Roberta Beep! Beep! I do not wish to be annihilated! I am a robot. It is my duty to serve a master. Beep! *You* will be my new master! Beep!

Santa Oh, Roberta! How could you!

Dame You two-faced tin lizzy, you!

Roberta (*moving nearer to Vileun*) I am yours to command, master. Beep! (*She bows to Vileun*)

Vileun (*turning to Astra*) Another robot would be most useful to us. (*To Roberta*) Agreed! (*He bends over her*) Consider yourself engaged.

Roberta grabs the amulet and rips it from Vileun's neck

A tremendous thunder clap is heard, followed by the loudest, weirdest noises imaginable. Dazzling lights flash across the stage—and audience—if possible. Vileun and Astra are held in an eerie green spotlight. They give the appearance of shrinking away to nothing

(*In a strangled voice, above the noise*) I've been foiled by a heap of tin!!

Vileun |
             | (*together*) Ahhhh!!
Astra |

There is a blinding flash, followed by a Black-out

Vileun and Astra's cries fade away as they exit under cover of darkness

When the lights return to normal Vileun and Astra have vanished from the scene

Dick They've gone!

All Hurray!

They all rush to Roberta

Tommy Roberta, you saved our lives!

Dame (*hugging and kissing Roberta*) Oh! You clever little cousin to a colander, you!

Santa (*laughing*) Careful, Dame Dangle! We don't want her to go rusty!

They all shake Roberta's hand and pat her on the head, etc.

The Monster enters with Crystal, the Villagers, the Children and the Varborites

Dick (*to the Monster, proudly*) Your Highness! Vileun the Vile has been destroyed!

All Hurray!

Roberta hands the amulet to the Monster and bows

Monster And what of Astra, the astrologer?

Dame Oh, we fixed her as well, your Royal Flush! She went off in the same puff of smoke!

Tommy Yes, you won't see her ugly mug again!

The Monster is obviously shaken by this news

Monster Oh, ... I see ...

Crystal What's the matter, your Highness?

Monster Astra was the only person with the power to change me back into my former self!

All (*horrified*) Oh, *no!*

Monster (*with a deep sigh*) It seems I shall have to remain a monster for ever.

All are downcast

Santa Your Highness, I have a little knowledge of magic. And I think I know one spell that might help you.

All (*ad lib*) Oh, try it! Try it, Santa, *etc.*

Santa (*moving to the Monster, thinking hard*) Now, let me see. I must get the words right. (*To the others*) Sh! Sh! (*He mumbles to himself*) Yes! That's it! (*He clears his throat, then casts a magic spell on the Monster*)
> Away with tails, scales and fur,
> We want to see you the way you were.
> Away with talons, tusks and mane,
> Return to us, as the Prince again!

Santa makes a magic pass at the Monster. There is a flash, followed by a Black-out

When the Lights come up, the Monster has gone and the handsome Prince Paragon stands in its place

Varborites (*giving their salute*) Prince Paragon!

Villagers Hurray! Good old Santa!

Prince Paragon examines himself with joy, and shakes Santa warmly by the hand

Prince My dear friend! (*To others*) All of you—what can I say? You have not only returned my planet to me, but my body as well. I know I speak for all the planets of the Universe when I say, thank you for ridding us of that foul usurper. How can I ever repay you?

Dick A safe journey home is all we ask, your Highness.

Prince My fastest space ship is at your disposal.

Dame (*groaning*) Oh, no! Can't we go home by bus!

Santa (*to Prince*) We'd better leave at once. It's Christmas on Earth next week and I've got a hundred and one things to deal with. (*He glances at Dick and Crystal then turns to Roberta*) Roberta, as it's just going to be the two of us this year, we shall have to put in some overtime.

Crystal (*moving to Santa*) But, Santa ...

Santa (*taking her hands*) I release you from your duties, my dear. (*He winks at Dick*) I'm sure you would rather be otherwise *engaged*.

Santa hands Crystal to Dick. They embrace, fondly

Null Your Highness, can I return to Earth with them! I rather fancy living there.

Prince You are free to do as you wish.

Void (*slipping his arm around Dame Dangle's waist*) I rather fancy it an' all!

Dame (*squealing with delight*) Ooo! You amorous astronut, you! Let's get down to Earth, before your boosters burst!

Song 17 (*All—Reprise*)

The main tabs close. The music continues. The taps re-open, almost immediately, to show the Village of Merrydale, ready for the finale walk down

The Company enter, and take their bows in the following order:

Varborites; Village Children; Villagers; Dancing Doll and Leader; Tommy, Monster and Prince; Astra; Null and Void; Vileun; Roberta; Dick and Crystal; Dame Dangle; Santa, carrying a sack of toys

If possible Santa could enter on a sleigh, pushed by the Village Children and Varborites. If more time is needed for finale costume changes, the Village Children and the Varborites could sing a reprise on their own at the beginning of the Finale

Dick	(*To the audience*) And so, dear friends, our story ends.
Crystal	We hope it gave you pleasure.
Astra	I've learnt my lesson, I'll make amends,
Dame	(*hugging Void*) And me, I've found a treasure!
Null	(*pointing to Void*) He always hid from UFOs.
Tommy	But that one's caught him proper!
Prince	She'll certainly keep him on his toes.
Void	(*with a grimace at Dame*) I think I've come a cropper!
Vileun	My plan to rule the Universe was foiled by that tin heap!
Roberta	Don't be rude, accept defeat, you nasty old—Beep! Beep!
Santa	We have enjoyed your company, it's time for us to leave,
	But don't forget, I'll see you all, again on Christmas Eve.
	I'll be coming down your chimneys, my sack full up with toys,
	There's lots of goodies hid in there for all you girls and boys.
	I hope you get the things you want, I try to get it right,
	Your letters are a help to me, so don't forget to write.
	(*Waving*) Good bye, and . . .
All	(*waving*) Merry Christmas!

Song 18 (*All*)

(*Suggestion: "We wish you a Merry Christmas"*)

CURTAIN

FURNITURE AND PROPERTY LIST

ACT I

SCENE 1

On stage: Tabs or front cloth

Off stage: Planet chart, report, large black book **(Astra)**

Personal: **Vileun** (throughout): amulet on chain, ray gun
Null (throughout) ray gun
Void (throughout) ray gun

SCENE 2

On stage: Village backcloth
Dame Dangle's cottage
Santa's House. *On it:* sign
Wall ground row
Tree wings

Off stage: Overcoat, top hat, scarf, carpet bag. *In it:* red Santa Claus coat **(Santa)**
Flying saucer

Personal: **1st Girl:** trick rag doll
Roberta: flower
Santa (throughout) Spectacles, apron. *In apron pocket:* oil can, ruler,
screw driver

SCENE 3

On stage: Tabs or front cloth

Off stage: Sweets for children in audience **(Null** and **Void)**

SCENE 4

On stage: Room backcloth
Room wings
Magic cabinet/rocket

Personal: **1st Girl:** trick rag doll
Roberta: toy space rocket

ACT II

SCENE 1

On stage: Interior of Rocket cloth
Rocket wings
Control console, computers etc.

Off stage: Space helmet **(Dame Dangle)**

Personal: **Dame** (throughout) Silver shoulder bag, silver space boots

SCENE 2

On stage: Tabs or front cloth

Off stage: Large cut-out of hand
Sweets for children in audience **(Dame Dangle** and **Void)**
Song sheet

Personal: **Void:** large handkerchief with hole

SCENE 3

On stage: Planet backcloth
Planet wings
Planet ground row

Personal: **Dame:** rock in boot
Roberta: small oil can

SCENE 4

On stage: Tabs or front cloth

Off stage: Tray with two "outer space" goblets **(Astra)**

Personal: **Dick:** small drug bottle

FINALE

On stage: As ACT I, Scene 2

Off stage: Large sack of toys **(Santa)**
Sleigh (optional)

LIGHTING PLOT

ACT I, SCENE 1

To open: Dim, "sinister" lighting

Cue 1   **Vileun:** "Destination—Earth! Ha! Ha! Ha!" Vileun exits   (Page 4)
             Fade to Black-out

ACT I, SCENE 2

To open: General external lighting

Cue 2   Noise of flying saucer grows   (Page 19)
             Stage darkens

Cue 3   Flying saucer arrives   (Page 19)
             Flashing lights

Cue 4   **Vileun:** "Now to find Santa Claus! Ha! Ha! Ha!"   (Page 19)
             Fade to Black-out

ACT I, SCENE 3

To open: General external lighting

Cue 5   **Null:** "Here goes!"   (Page 21)
             House lights up

Cue 6   **Null** and **Void** return to stage   (Page 21)
             House lights down

Cue 7   **Vileun** exits   (Page 24)
             Fade to Black-out

ACT I, SCENE 4

To open: General interior lighting

Cue 8   **Dick:** ". . . We might still be in time to save Santa!"   (Page 28)
             Glowing light floods stage from left, gradually fading

Cue 9   **All:** "Hocus Pocus!!!"   (Page 29)
             A flash; Black-out; then, when rocket is set, lights up

ACT II, SCENE 1

To open: General interior lighting: Flashing lights on control console

Cue 10   **Roberta:** "We are under attack!"   (Page 33)
             "Weird" flashing lights replace general lighting; as noise fades
             the lights return to normal

Cue 11   **Dame:** "... I'm too young to die!!"   (Page 34)
            Flashing lights and, as noise reaches climax, flash followed by
            Black-out

ACT II, SCENE 2

To open: General interior lighting

Cue 12   **Null** grabs **Void** and hauls him out   (Page 41)
            Fade to Black-out

ACT II, SCENE 3

To open: Bluish lighting, exterior

Cue 13   The cast gather around **Dick**   (Page 47)
            Fade to Black-out

ACT II, SCENE 4

To open: General interior lighting

Cue 14   Thunderclap   (Page 53)
            Dazzling lights flash across stage, green spot on Vileun and Astra

Cue 15   **Vileun** and **Astra:** "Ahhhhh!!"   (Page 53)
            Flash followed by Black-out. After a pause lights up to normal

Cue 16   **Santa** makes a magic pass at the **Monster**   (Page 54)
            Flash followed by Black-out. After a pause lights up to normal

EFFECTS PLOT

ACT I

SCENE 1

Cue 1   As curtain opens   (Page 1)
          Weird, "sinister" noises, ground mist

SCENE 2

Cue 2   **Dame** creeps into the house   (Page 8)
          Loud crash

Cue 3   **Dame:** "What's that? . . . Ooo! Ah!"   (Page 8)
          Loud bang, followed by flash

Cue 4   After all have exited, a pause   (Page 19)
          Noise of flying saucer, gradually getting louder

Cue 5   Flying saucer arrives   (Page 19)
          Smoke and flashes

SCENE 4

Cue 6   **Dick:** ". . . We might still be in time to save Santa!"   (Page 28)
          Noise of flying saucer taking off

Cue 7   **All:** "Hocus Pocus!!!"   (Page 29)
          Flash

ACT II

SCENE 1

Cue 8   As curtain opens   (Page 30)
          Console emits flashes and noises

Cue 9   **Roberta:** ". . . We are under attack!"   (Page 33)
          Space battle noises

Cue 10 **Dame:** "Oo! I'm too young to die!"   (Page 34)
          Whine, smoke, bang and flash as console explodes

Cue 11 In Black-out   (Page 34)
          Explosion

SCENE 3

Cue 12 As curtain opens   (Page 41)
          Eerie music, mist

Cue 13   **Varborites:** "True!"   (Page 41)
            Monster's roar

Cue 14   **All** get to their feet   (Page 42)
            Monster's roar

Cue 15   **2nd Varborite:** "Before something else does!"   (Page 43)
            Monster's roar

Scene 4

Cue 16   **Roberta** grabs the amulet from **Vileun**'s neck   (Page 53)
            Thunderclap, followed by loud, weird noises

Cue 17   **Vileun** and **Astra:** "Ahhhhh!"   (Page 53)
            Flash

Cue 18   **Santa** makes a magic pass at the **Monster**   (Page 54)
            Flash

MADE AND PRINTED IN GREAT BRITAIN BY
LATIMER TREND & COMPANY LTD, PLYMOUTH
MADE IN ENGLAND